CW01497671

*The Gobshite
Guidebook*

Jarlath Regan is a stand-up comedian, podcaster and gobshite expert. Not only has he worked with thousands of them over the years, he also narrowly escaped permanent gobshite status by marrying a woman with tremendous amounts of patience and cop on. His viral Instagram and TikTok sketches about modern life and the Irish Mammy have earned him millions of views and subscribers. Today he appears regularly on television, tours the world performing his one-man stand-up shows and offers advice to anyone who will listen about how they can cope with the gobshites in their lives.

Instagram: **@jarlathregan__irishmanabroad**

Jarlath's gobshite-free online safe space: **www.jigser.com**

'I've long admired Jarlath Regan as a wry comedy stylist and astute podcaster but after this amusing, eye-opening exposé of gobshites it is for his valuable public service that we should be forever grateful.'

ARDAL O'HANLON

The Gobshite Guidebook

A SURVIVAL MANUAL

JARLATH REGAN

GILL BOOKS

Gill Books

Hume Avenue

Park West

Dublin 12

www.gillbooks.ie

Gill Books is an imprint of M.H. Gill and Co.

978 18045 8317 3

Designed by Luke Doyle

Edited by Liza Costello

Proofread by Jane Rogers

Printed and bound in the UK using 100% renewable electricity
at CPI Group (UK) Ltd

This book is typeset in English Grotesque.

The paper used in this book comes from the wood pulp of sustainably managed forests.

*To the best of our knowledge, this book complies in full with the requirements of the
General Product Safety Regulation (GPSR). For further information and help with
any safety queries, please contact us at productsafety@gill.ie.*

A CIP catalogue record for this book is available from
the British Library.

5 4 3 2 1

Contents

Introduction

Gobshites: every family, WhatsApp group, workplace and team has one. If you think yours doesn't then it could be you or someone very close to you. Either way, you definitely need to read this book. Gobshites are a fact of life and a feature of every period in human history. From the first gobshite who tried to eat fire to the influencer gobshites who seriously hurt themselves making parkour videos on TikTok, gobshites are everywhere. Their existence is such a challenge that many would rather not speak of them for the sake of a peaceful life. This approach is foolish and actually creates more problems; gobshites don't just demand our attention, they demand detailed explanations of things that everyone else can grasp on sight. Over the last few years, the 'ignore that gobshite' approach has cost insurance companies millions. The gobshite situation facing the world today is getting worse, not better.

The world's gobshite population is a time sponge. These people soak up so much of our time that a guidebook examining their behaviour, history and psychology has never been written. They simply haven't allowed us the time. By continuously asking productive people questions, like 'What are ya doing?', 'Does anyone else hear that buzzing?' and 'How come the sun doesn't burn away the clouds?', they have ruined some of the world's greatest projects, including a gobshite guidebook. Up to now, others who attempted to write a book of this nature met one of two fates: they either became so involved with the gobshites they studied that their writing time evaporated and the project was never completed; or the publisher to whom the concept of a gobshite guidebook was presented had one or two gobshites working there who failed to understand the concept and stood in its way. Ironically, if those publishers had had this book in their hands they might have found a way of evading, placating or pushing past the gobshites in their lives. I am therefore massively grateful to those in Gill Books involved in the publication of this book, for ignoring and fobbing off the gobshites they work with who questioned the need for it.

Gobshites think people who are quietly working on something are either sulking, being weird or ignoring them, and therefore feel compelled to do all they can to disrupt whatever the person happens to be working on. It is safe to say that keeping gobshites at bay was one of the most difficult tasks involved in the creative process of writing this book.

WHY YOU NEED THIS BOOK

Encountering a gobshite is an unavoidable part of our daily lives. From the gobshite on their phone behind the wheel of their car, oblivious to the difficulties they're causing the road users behind them, to the gobshite in the coffee shop using the same cloth to clean the tables and dry the cups, every single day can feel like one long gobshite obstacle course. The purpose of this book is to help you cope with them, understand them and feel less alone when confronted by one.

CONSIDER THIS BOOK YOUR GOBSHITE SNIFFER DOG

Eejits are harmless, gobshites can be dangerous! Is it possible to protect oneself from gobshites? We are never completely protected but we can lessen their impact. We can avoid finding ourselves in a position where a gobshite has responsibility at a significant moment in our lives, whether that be getting our first mortgage, acting as character witness in court or getting to the airport in time for a crucial flight. This guidebook will help you to sniff out gobshites hiding in plain sight. Since the pandemic, Brexit and certain elections, gobshites have been emboldened. They are now as omnipresent as social media – which incidentally is their favourite form of communication. If we can't avoid them, we must learn to live alongside them, tip-toe around them or run in the opposite direction.

The Gobshite Guidebook is a gift to everyone who has ever facepalmed or rolled their eyes, punched a cushion or bitten into their fist as a result of dealing with a gobshite in the wild. It is my dream that it will act as a ray of hope for those who have felt alone in dealing with such people, and as an instructive manual for those who are just now encountering a gobshite for the first time, and perhaps feeling that a bleak future lies ahead. There is also the distant hope that perhaps a gobshite may actually read this book, see themselves in it and have a moment where they grasp the hardship they are causing their family, friends, colleagues and society. As you will learn in the coming pages, that is a completely unrealistic dream.

IDENTIFYING GOBSHITES IN THE WILD

Gobshite characteristics are easy to spot. For example:

- Is he saying the words, 'Why is everyone so uptight?'
- Is he laughing hysterically at one of his own jokes?
- Is he an adult attempting to dominate a child in a game of football?
- Is he tailgating you in a German saloon car?
- Is he pronouncing it 'pacifically'?
- Is she refusing to take off her boots at airport security?
- Is he taking up a bench at the gym texting on his phone for half an hour?
- Is he claiming to know the owner?
- Is he wearing sunglasses indoors?
- Did she just skip you at the bar?
- Did he just mansplain childbirth?

If your answer to any of these is 'yes', you may be in the presence of a gobshite. Read on for advice on how to deal with them.

Are Gobshites Born That Way?

Wives of gobshites spend much of their week rubbing their temples asking some pretty existential questions while another gobshite crisis unfolds. When their husband flies into a blind panic when he can't find his wallet, they ask whether he has looked for the wallet. Then they grin and bear it as their gobshite husband gets angrier and angrier. They watch as he cancels his credit cards. The wife of the gobshite then locates the missing wallet behind a cushion on the chair on which her beloved usually sits. The wife of the gobshite then retires to the downstairs bathroom and wonders aloud while gripping the sink, 'How did I wind up married to this gobshite?', 'Why is he like this?' and 'What went wrong in his upbringing to produce an adult gobshite such as this?' Beneath these questions lies one bigger concern – 'Is being a complete and utter gobshite hereditary or is it a pattern of learned behaviour?'

Many believe that every human is born a gobshite. For the first five years of a child's life, gobshite behaviour is not just normal and acceptable, it is even celebrated by doting parents. A child staring vacantly into the distance for extended periods is said to be 'thinking'. A grown-up doing the same thing is seen as vacant, gawping and slack-jawed –

a person on screensaver mode. A toddler expects others should take care of them and we love it. But a man in his thirties who wants his mammy to pick him up from the station is a man-child gobshite who can't be trusted to call a taxi.

Grabbing things they don't own, spilling food and drinks, shouting for no reason, soiling themselves in public, talking gobbledygook and making decisions that put their lives in danger – toddlers are gobshites but we find their terrible behaviour lovable. We savour even their worst moments as treasured memories. We laugh when they cause a fuss or show a complete lack of understanding of how the world works. 'He tried to eat the play dough!' 'She thinks the teacher lives in the school.' 'He asked if he could go to space on holidays.'

According to the 'gobshites are born that way' school of thought, while most people leave behind their gobshite chrysalis and blossom into fully functioning, thoughtful adults, some do not. It's a convincing argument, especially when we consider the teenage years. One 13-year-old can invent revolutionary technology as another derives joy from punching their friends in the bollocks. One teenager can produce great works of art while another regularly winds up in hospital because they keep forgetting about their peanut allergy. Most of us learn somewhere along the way not to put our fingers into electrical sockets, while others try to shove their penis into toasters 'for a laugh'.

But what of the teen who changes from a thoughtful, warm-hearted and diligent youngster to the type of gobshite that antagonises stray dogs? Most of us know of a thoroughbred gobshite teenager who could be relied upon to babysit as an eight-year-old child but now, as a young adult, can barely be trusted with scissors. It boggles parents' minds to remember that these teens, who are now so committed to the gobshite way of life, were once children who regularly made cupcakes on Saturday afternoons. How do we account for the child who at seven years old enjoys nature documentaries and writing in their journal, yet at 14 nearly burns a house down because they were attempting to light their own farts?

Are gobshites born or does a person learn to be a gobshite? Maybe two things can be true at the same time. It seems that there are those with a gobshite gene or predisposition to gobshite behaviour, and those who follow the leader. Not every kid walks into pre-school and decides to eat the sand in the play pit. Some only eat the sand after seeing another gobshite toddler attempt it. It's understandable that some people grow up to be gobshites when their only role models are also gobshites.

We hear it all the time: 'That young lad is an awful gobshite. Is it any wonder? Have you met his father? The brother is no different.' The influence of gobshites on regular, well-adjusted people is so malignant that just about anyone can be turned into one in a relatively short period of time. That's how mobs are formed. That's how football hooliganism works. Not everyone in the marauding pack of yobs abroad is a gobshite. They've just been swept along by the infectious energy and magnetic nature of idiotic impulsivity.

THE COLD, HARD TRUTH

Puzzling over why a gobshite is the way they are, or where they came from and why, is a maddening and never-ending rabbit hole that you go down at your peril. We have all lain awake in bed wondering why a near or distant relative is such a gobshite. This is the raison d'être of this guidebook.

Gobshites are innovators. Finding new and inventive methods to do simple tasks in the most upsetting ways is their gift. In this instance a gobshite has been told by his wife that that his continuous failure to replace empty toilet rolls is sending her into fits of rage. Rather than changing the toilet roll as normal, this gobshite has managed to conjure up a new way to both replace the roll and anger his wife to a new level. In the ensuing argument he will inflame matters by telling her she needs to 'chillax'.

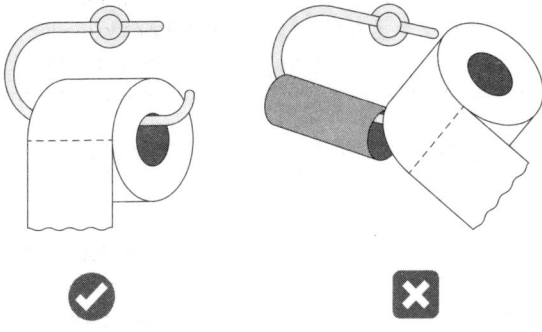

It is unwise to dwell on the how or why of the existence of gobshites. Our focus should be on what we know for sure about this group of life-ruining dicks, the challenges they present us with and the steps we can take to protect ourselves from them. Being ill-prepared for the gobshites in your life is a dangerous path that can leave you looking foolish or, worse, result in others grouping you in with the gobshites. Let us begin.

Dealing with Gobshites: Coping Mechanisms

Interacting with a known gobshite is difficult enough in a working environment, such as the office, or on public transport. It calls upon a resourcefulness that not everyone possesses. Those related to, married to or forced to work with gobshites have developed coping strategies to help them through the day.

HIDING IN THE TOILETS

The toilet is the panic room for those dealing with gobshites on a daily basis. It offers seclusion and refuge from the challenge of coping with the gobshite. In the past, many have pondered over why lavatory manufacturers have included a toilet seat cover as standard on their products. Is it to protect the world from the stinks within the bowl? Is it to conceal the sound of the flush? The seat cover was in fact designed for users to sit on while clawing at their eyes as they ask, 'How am I related to this gobshite?'

LONG WALKS

Walkers will tell you that walking has tremendous health benefits, but in truth, the activity of walking somewhere for no reason was invented by relatives of gobshites. The first person to go on a gobshite-induced long walk never intended to return. They had had it up to their neck with the nonsense of a gobshite and thought, 'Fuck this, I'm out of here.' They left the building and took off like Forrest Gump. Over the course of the walk they realised that they couldn't just leave their family, responsibilities and car keys. So they returned. In typical nosy gobshite fashion, the first long walker was asked, 'Where did you go?' The blurted-out answer? 'I just went for a long walk.' The long walk became a destination for all long-term sufferers of gobshites across the world.

STARING OUT THE WINDOW WHILE RUBBING YOUR FACE

When a long walk is not an option, many who are forced to endure gobshites will take to staring out a window dreaming of being somewhere else. Window staring can be combined with toilet seat sitting for maximum effect. The larger the landscape and broader the horizon, the more therapeutic the gaze can feel. Rubbing of the temples, forehead and eyes has been known to enhance the soothing quality of the window stare. The greatest challenge posed to a gobshite-induced window stare is the inevitable interruption by a gobshite. Due to their inability to reflect or meditate, gobshites find any form of silent contemplation bizarre and unusual. Window stares are frequently interrupted by gobshites asking, 'What are ya lookin' at?', 'What's out the window?', 'Are you going mad?' and 'What's wrong with ya?' Remember to breathe.

DRINKING ALCOHOL

Resorting to alcohol to cope with the strain of a gobshite is the least advisable of all the coping strategies, for many reasons. While it is tempting to numb yourself to their behaviours, pouring alcohol on a gobshite problem is like throwing petrol on the flames. In many cases, as your intoxication level rises, your tolerance level lowers. Arguments you would never normally engage in with a gobshite suddenly become life-or-death debates once alcohol is in the system. Avoid alcohol at all costs when dealing with a gobshite. If at all possible, keep it away from them as well. Alcohol is an accelerant for all the worst gobshite behaviours.

4

The Effect of Alcohol on Gobshites

'I thought this was meant to be a party!'

'Why did you bring us to a bar if you didn't want me to get drunk?'

'It's a wedding! It's normal for a few things to get broken.'

If you've heard any of these phrases, you've already experienced the dangerous combination of alcohol and gobshitery. Gobshites will always make out that their inability to drink in moderation is somehow both a virtue and something that you should have expected and accounted for. Their drunken rampages are exceptionally tricky to navigate because they don't view their behaviour as problematic. They see themselves as entertaining and worthy of praise, something you would surely see too if only you had a better sense of craic or fun in you.

WHY GOBSHITES LOVE ALCOHOL

Drinking alcohol lowers inhibitions and makes everyone a little dumber, slower on the uptake and more prone to poor choices. As such, for a gobshite alcohol is the perfect drug, in that it makes them feel more normal. It levels the playing field and acts as a get-out-of-jail-free card for their worst episodes. If everyone is hammered, the gobshite's poor moral

Effect of Alcohol on Gobshites

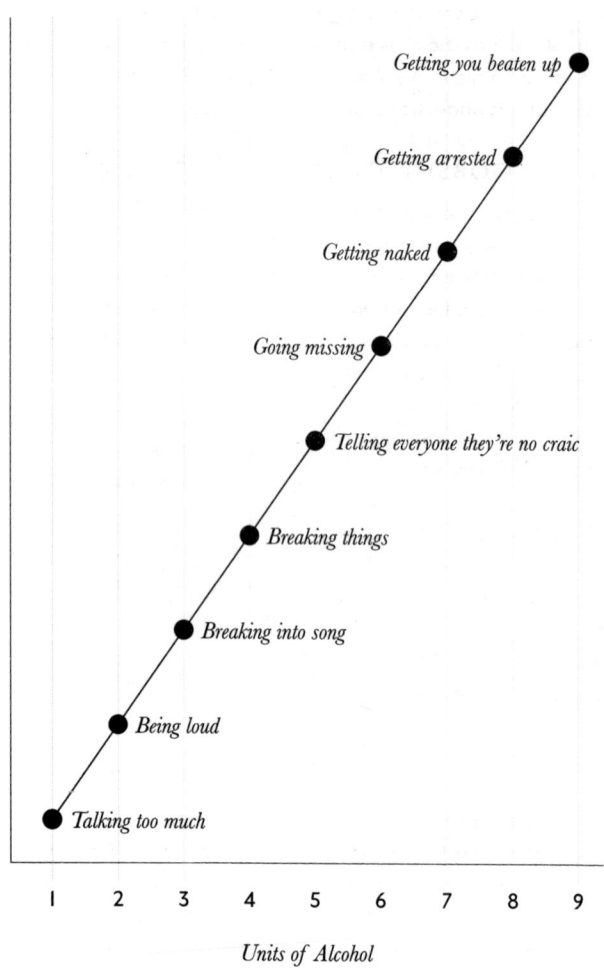

Getting you beaten up

Getting arrested

Getting naked

Going missing

Telling everyone they're no craic

Breaking things

Breaking into song

Being loud

Talking too much

1 2 3 4 5 6 7 8 9

Units of Alcohol

compass can be explained away. When everyone is drinking, the broken television, lamp or dog flap might have occurred as a result of someone else rather than them. Through the prism of being shit-faced, a gobshite who is a gobshite 24/7 can blend into the crowd of people who have chosen to act a bit silly for a night. A gobshite would never consciously know this, but it is understood on a deeper level.

GOBSHITES ON A NIGHT OUT

When a gobshite says they are going 'out for the night', this can only mean one thing: trouble for everyone connected to them. A gobshite does not think they had a night out unless there was some form of drama. They regard evenings spent uneventfully drinking a few pints, chatting and watching a match on the TV as a 'waste of time'. They may even get angry and refer to those they are drinking with as 'dry shites' simply because they have refused to go to a nightclub with them on a Tuesday.

Trying to reason with a gobshite who wants a 'proper night out' when you have work the next day is an actual waste of time. Once a gobshite has decided they are going to have a night out, whether or not you approve is irrelevant. The fact that it is your wedding, big exam or mother's funeral the next day is also irrelevant.

Those who know what it's like to have a gobshite friend who loves a 'proper night out' can often find themselves forced to act as a gobshite shepherd on these evenings. Your role is as a kind of minder for the gobshite. Your primary function is to stop them climbing railings, arguing with strangers, skipping queues in takeaways or handing their phone and wallet to complete strangers. Gobshite shepherd is a thankless role that the siblings of gobshites will know all too well. In the case of a brother or sister who is a gobshite, the shepherd endures the night out through a constant state of vigilance, worry and anxiety over what is coming next. A person in this position is more like the minder of an alcoholic rock star. You know there will be one or more incidents on the night out; all you're trying to do is anticipate them and prevent your gobshite from vanishing out a window or into a strange vehicle.

THE AFTERMATH OF A GOBSHITE 'NIGHT OUT'

The saddest part is that if anything happens to the gobshite you are attempting to shepherd, the following day you will receive all the blame for having allowed it to occur. 'Why did you let me buy rounds for everyone in the bar? I thought you were meant to be looking out for me. What did you do with my phone?' That is not to say that gobshites will not receive blowback for their actions.

Here are some sentences often used by gobshites when partners, parents or the police are investigating what happened the night before. Put a little tick next to each sentence you have heard from the gobshites in your life.

☐ *Ah come on, how was I to know you weren't allowed to climb the railings? I was drunk!*

☐ *You're asking me like I'm supposed to remember things that happen when I'm shitfaced. I think you're being really hard on me.*

☐ *They served me the pints. The rest is history. Why am I being blamed for a having a good time?*

Is being drunk a crime now? Well, excuse me for having a good time.

That party was like a funeral until I got there. Was I supposed to sit in the corner like the rest of ye dry shites?

I didn't hear what he said to me. That's why I punched him. He knew I was drunk. Why was he trying to ask me a question, like?

Am I expected to calculate the cost of the damage I'm doing while I'm drunk? Come on, lads. I'm trying to have a good time, for God's sake.

Gobshites who ruin events as a direct result of being too drunk tend to have a version of what happened that paints them as the saviour rather than the destroyer of the moment. It's hard for non-gobshites to comprehend how far from reality these distortions can be and how adamantly the gobshite will stick to them.

5

Celebrity Gobshites

Not all gobshites are a complete disaster. Some are billionaires. Many have landed big jobs. History is littered with tasks gone disastrously wrong because they were assigned to a gobshite. The detrimental impact of gobshites on human progress is vast. Their influence upon people can be mesmerising. The success of gobshites is a constant source of wonder globally. 'How did that gobshite get into the Oval Office?', 'How the hell has that gobshite managed to stay alive, never mind win an Oscar?' The successful gobshite usually has tremendous resilience and thicker than thick skin. They do not hear criticism when it is directed at them (Piers Morgan). They even see the fact they're being criticised as a positive sign (Katie Hopkins and Nigel Farage). The impactful gobshite often enjoys being the villain and will say things like 'There's no such thing as bad publicity.' Here's a few really successful proven gobshites you might know.

ELON MUSK – INVENTOR, BUSINESS MOGUL, INFLUENCER AND GOBSHITE

Elon is a great example of a gobshite others will claim is not a gobshite because he is wealthy. Can gobshites be rich? Of course they can. The world is full of gobshites who managed to become rich only to lose it all. Elon is clearly in the middle of his rise and fall story.

'But didn't he invent an electric car or something?' Did he, though? How many Tesla inventions have his actual gobshite fingerprints on them? He owns the research facility, but does he do the research? My guess is that the success of the Elon Musk business empire is down to a few key gobshite wranglers: men and women who distract Elon when he's about to make a catastrophic decision or perform an elaborate charade to give him the impression he is the brains of the operation. I'd imagine that once a month Elon arrives into the facility wearing a white coat and spectacles, wanting to 'do some inventing'. The gobshite gurus have a procedure that kicks into action immediately. They set him up with an assistant at a laptop and a few interns carrying notebooks. Elon is then encouraged to run his mouth off about whatever vehicle he dreamt about or a thing he thinks 'could be cool'. The interns then frantically scribble notes while saying things like, 'so cool' and 'this is great, Elon', and winking to one another theatrically. Musk leaves around 11 a.m. and they return to working on the actual technology while he signs some cheques next door.

KANYE WEST – ARTIST, MUSICIAN, DESIGNER AND GOBSHITE

Unlike a gobshite like Elon Musk, Kanye or Ye actually has talent and a creative ability that gets scuppered by his gobshite tendency to make wild statements and upset people who previously liked or helped him. Like most gobshites, he is then perplexed by the fallout from the choices he has made. 'People are too sensitive nowadays' is a gobshite phrase he uses regularly, which loosely translates as 'I should be allowed to say whatever I like without any concern for the feelings of others.' Kanye didn't always think this. Like a lot of gobshites who were once normal people, he became the victim of his own success. In this sense, he's very similar to the apprentice builder on site who gets one compliment on his workmanship from the foreman and immediately asks for a pay raise.

KATIE HOPKINS – GOBSHITE AND INFLUENCER I GUESS

Katie is the type of gobshite who would argue with you over laughter being a good thing. She is a contrarian gobshite who has found success by playing devil's advocate when nobody needed to hear the other side. She doesn't believe much of what she has to say, she just likes the idea of saying things and people listening. A lot like the gobshite in your local pub who refuses to admit Ronaldo is a good football player, Katie is the type of gobshite that has confused being oppositional with dogged determination. She seems to think that holding a hurtful opinion makes her more interesting and courageous. Most of all, she finds it funny when people get upset with her. That's a very unusual type of gobshite. Most gobshites are confused as to why there is so much anger directed towards them. Katie Hopkins knows exactly why. It's the things she says and how she says them. And yet she is, at the time of writing, on a sellout tour of the UK and Ireland saying the unsayable. Being outrageous just to be outrageous is the newest type of gobshite behaviour. Keep an eye out for it.

THE GOBSHITE ENTITLEMENT THRESHOLD

The more a gobshite pays for a product or service, the more they feel entitled to complain/whinge. This graph shows the incremental rise based on price and the point at which gobshite complaints tail off. This steep decline is due to the number of wealthy gobshites who are more focused on blowing all their income as fast possible rather than getting any sort of value for it. This is known as the Gobshite Entitlement Threshold. The complaint numbers return to the average level until the wealthy gobshite inevitably loses all their money.

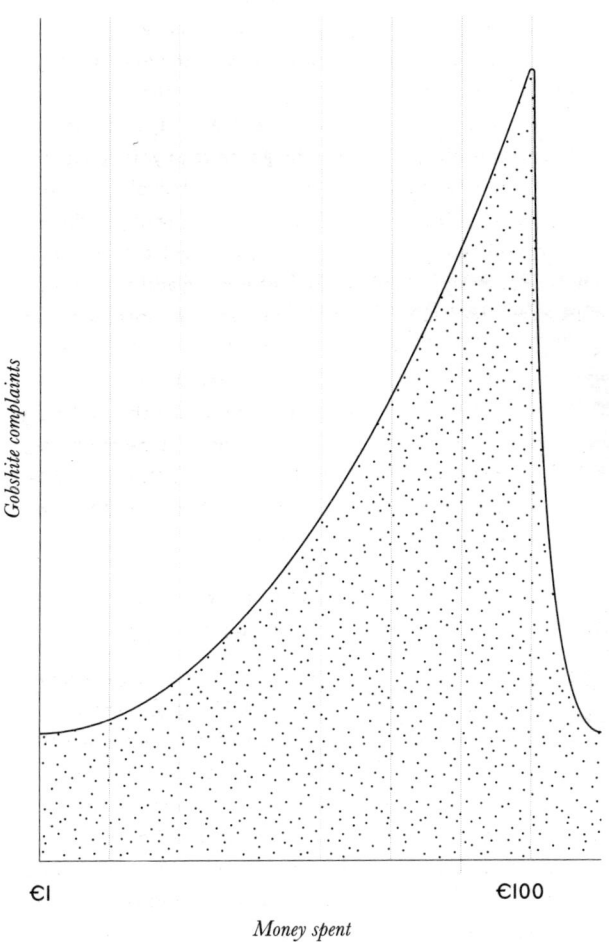

Do Gobshites Know They Are Gobshites?

Sadly, no. Gobshites lack the self-awareness needed to be able to see themselves for what they are. The inability to understand the pain, anxiety, fury and difficulty they are causing everyone around them is a key characteristic of a gobshite. If a person says, 'I'm sorry if this whole thing has upset you in any way,' they are not a gobshite. A gobshite has never apologised in advance, asked 'Is this a good time?', or felt bad for the person who has had to leave work to help them get their head unstuck from some railings. A gobshite never sees the difficulty they are causing others and can therefore never feel remorse. That's a hard one to get your head around as a non-gobshite. All we see is the pain, the frustration, the broken radiator you told them not to sit on, the stain on the carpet from their vomit, the scrape they put on the ceiling when they were jumping on your bed swinging a hurl. How can a gobshite be completely blind to the fact that they are a gobshite?

Some say it is a mystery as old as time. How can a gobshite's view of themselves be so disconnected from how the world sees them? How can a person who elicits this much anger – from bus drivers, bouncers, passers-by, other road users, members of the opposite sex and even animals – be blissfully unaware of how others perceive them? And if they can't see how others see them, how *do* they see themselves?

Your Gobshite Might See Themselves As ...

THE ONLY ONE LEFT WHO IS UP FOR THE CRAIC

The majority of the gobshites with major issues around not making a complete show of themselves at public or family events see themselves as crusaders for 'the craic'. They're the last man standing from the years when people had a sense of humour. These gobshites believe themselves to be on a mission of some sort to remind people how to have 'fun'. Fun, in their eyes, constitutes anything that others would view as unmannerly or inappropriate behaviour. Stealing drinks from other tables in a bar, hiding fish down the back of a couch, laughing loudly as a funeral cortège passes, throwing someone's new shoes on the roof of their house, eating foods or drinking beverages reserved for a special event, indecent exposure, assaulting you on your 39th birthday while shouting 'birthday beating!' The unshakable belief that they are the last of the fun people in the world is only reinforced by those who tell them to stop or explain that now is not a good time for a group sing-song. The only thing that reinforces the belief more than a voice of reason is another gobshite. Like dogs spotting each other from a distance, gobshites who see themselves as the 'defenders of the craic' lock eyes from across a crowded room and form an instant friendship. Ever ask two gobshites how they know each other? They never have an answer.

THE VICTIM

Not all gobshites are seeking to liven up every event they attend. Many gobshites move through the world leaving a trail of destruction behind them without getting drunk, whooping and hollering or crashing a funeral they have no business attending. The gobshite with a victim complex is making a mess of everything they touch by not taking the time to read the instructions, listen to the safety tutorial or even look at how everyone else around them is operating the petrol pump. This type of gobshite has a hangdog appearance and elicits sympathy from those who are unaware that this the fifteenth time this person has dropped their phone in the toilet. The gobshite who views himself as being very hard done by, or the victim of a system that failed to take him into consideration, is the most infuriating of all because no matter what disaster he causes, he can't comprehend how his lack of basic common sense is at the centre of it. 'Give me a break.' 'Why are you getting so mad at me?' 'Ah here, I tried my best to get the key to turn, how was I to know it would break in the door if I turned it like that?' This kind of person sees himself as sharing the same fate as the Birmingham Six, Steven Avery from *Making a Murderer* or Andy Dufresne from *The Shawshank Redemption*. They see themselves as good men with the worst luck.

THE MOST THOUGHTFUL PERSON

Hard as it is to believe, many gobshites see themselves as a thoughtful kind of person. They might set fire to the house trying to recreate some candlelit scene they saw in a movie, or destroy their clothes by forgetting there was bleach in the bath, but that's not the point. In their eyes, they were trying their best. It's not their fault your dog is too stupid to be let off the lead. The gobshite who sees himself as the world's 'best guy' thinks that because he made an effort he can't be penalised for the outcome. The gobshite with the 'I was only trying to do something nice' mentality thinks that nobody really appreciates them. They fail to see that a thoughtful act is not a thoughtful act if it creates more hassle, anxiety and damage than not doing it at all. Many of these types of gobshites also see themselves as victims. They believe that their best intentions should be appreciated and that another, less uptight person would see the well-meaning nature of what they did. Not that the house burned down or that the dog got run over.

THE SMARTEST GUY IN THE ROOM

I know. It is remarkable to think that many of these gobshites, who cost us all this time and energy, ruin our holidays, infuriate us on the roads and generally make our lives more difficult, think that they are the smartest people in the world. Unfortunately, it is true. The unfounded gobshite confidence is the most flabbergasting thing in the world. How can someone this thick think that they know better than everyone else? How can someone who has failed time and time again to see imminent danger think that they should be the safety officer on site? How can someone who has bankrupted themselves half a dozen times think that they are an authority on finance? The answer is simple: they are a gobshite. The inability to see their own flaws is central to that identity. A gobshite is a person with food on their face who tells you your table manners leave a lot to be desired. A gobshite is a person whose idea of parenting is locking their kid in their room on an Xbox, and then tells you that your own kid is out of control. There's a wilful ignorance to all gobshites. Those who think they are smarter than everyone else, in spite of all the evidence to the contrary, are among the most dangerous. The absence of an inner critic makes them superb in interviews. If you can't see your mistakes in

the past, if they don't register on your radar, you sound like
your whole life has been one long stream of successes.

Spotting a gobshite who sees himself as the smartest guy
in the room can be hard to do if you only speak to them
about their past. This is why recruiters ask for references.
The blind spot of the gobshite who sees himself as God's gift
concerns his (lack of) understanding of the impact of his
behaviour on other people. To them their last job was a cake
walk. A position they didn't find challenging enough so they
moved on. To their boss, having them around was a fucking
nightmare. To their co-workers, the entire time this gobshite
worked with them was one long ass-covering mission. They
did the gobshite's work for them because the gobshite failed
to see the work that needed to be done or did such a ham-
fisted job of their tasks that they all needed to be redone
later that day.

Gobshites never confess to being gobshites. They might even
try to bond with you about people they think are gobshites.
It's the number one way they fly under the radar. When a
gobshite finds someone who others agree is a pain in the ass
or who has made crucial mistakes, they will pile on to distract
from their own fuck-ups. Next time someone starts telling
you what a gobshite someone else is, be careful. You might be
talking to the worst kind of gobshite there is.

Knowing Your Eejits from Your Gobshites

Gobshites are like other people's silent farts. You don't know they are there until it's too late. Just like bad smells are often incorrectly identified as farts, many innocent people have been labelled gobshites. An eejit – stemming from the British term idiot – is far more common than a gobshite. Most people have it in them to be an eejit. 'Oh I'm such an eejit, I forgot to put the cat out.' We all do eejit-like things each day. 'I can't believe it. I'm such an eejit for putting the washing out today. I saw the forecast this morning. What was I thinking?'

Eejits make harmless mistakes like getting your drinks order wrong. Gobshites make errors that ruin your entire night, like inviting some lad they met in the toilet back to your house. Eejits can do kind things: 'You're some eejit, you didn't need to get me flowers.' Being an eejit is not a 24/7 state of existence. It has a transient quality. You can be a serious business person who likes to act the eejit on a night out. 'I saw you two acting the eejit on the dance floor. What are ye like?' But there's a permanence to being a gobshite that is somewhat tragic. We couldn't name every eejit in our lives, but if you try to think about the gobshites in your circle, you can name them all. Gobshites have no way back. They will always revert to being a gobshite at the worst possible times. That's where the expression 'Once a gobshite, always a gobshite' comes from.

REMEMBER: *An eejit is not a static state of existence. You can formerly be an eejit and move to a higher state of being. You may have heard an interaction such as this: 'Remember Sean? God almighty, what an fecking eejit he was. What's he up to now? He works for Google.' Gobshites, unlike eejits, are stuck as they are. Hence the expression, 'Once a gobshite, always a gobshite.'*

People are in a rush to make judgements today. Pigeon-holing people quickly has so many casualties. Just as someone who writes one good song gets labelled a musical genius, lads who get themselves locked in a toilet once get unfairly branded as gobshites. As a result, each year thousands of eejits will become known as gobshites. This has to stop. Finding clarity on the differences between a humble eejit and a full-blown gobshite is a key life skill that should be taught in school and on pre-marriage courses.

FINDING THE GOBSHITES IN YOUR LIFE IS EASY

Here are eight simple questions you can ask to help establish if a person in your life is a dangerous gobshite or a harmless eejit. Don't ask the gobshite directly. Just observe them in the wild, take notes and draw your own conclusions.

1) *Do they regularly say the sentence, 'How was I supposed to know that!'?*
   Gobshites believe their ignorance is the norm and that the world is an unpredictable place. They move from

one calamity to the next learning absolutely nothing in the process. 'How was I supposed to know that?' is their go-to line because they feel genuinely aggrieved when facing a consequence of their own actions – because it wasn't spelled out to them beforehand. For example, a bus departing at a fixed time. How were they supposed to know that? The bus timetable available online or at the bus stop? The instructions you printed out and gave them? The group of people who got on the bus ahead of them? The bus driver who asked them to their face if they wanted to get on? The gobshite assumes that any mistake they make is down to other people not taking sufficient account of their inability to do basic shit like everyone else.

2) *Are they confused by rules on health and safety?*
   Most gobshites can't understand simple codes of conduct even when they are explained to them. They have trouble fitting in because their own standards for behaviour rarely take into account the feelings or activities of others. They view rules such as weight limits, speed limits and 'no go' safety areas as silly or 'political correctness gone mad'. Keep an eye out for this at all times. The gobshite will rarely face punishment for allowing the warehouse to be robbed. You will, for letting a known gobshite lock up the main door.

3) *Do they make short-term mistakes others have to cope with long term?*
   An eejit will get you the wrong drink. A gobshite will return to your table with a drink for themselves and a group of people you've never met, who you are now expected to talk to for the rest of the night. They live in the here and now. This doesn't mean they are enlightened

or have achieved a Zen-like consciousness. It means that they can't anticipate issues even five minutes down the road. They are regularly the cause of food poisoning. They are the reason insurance premiums are so high. If you have a baby who refuses to sleep, they are the ones shouting at a television in the next room.

4) *Is their phone number always changing?*
Telecommunications pose a major issue for all gobshites. From the etiquette of knowing when is a good time to text to the simple task of owning and taking care of a mobile phone, it's a fraught experience. Gobshites believe everyone is suffering through the same turmoil on a daily basis. They believe phones are too small and slippery, the screens are 'too flimsy' and that the 'find my phone' function is the most-used app on everyone's phone. Gobshites' phone numbers have changed multiple times because they struggle to sustain anything that requires upkeep.

5) *Are people regularly angry with them for reasons they find hard to understand?*
'What? What did I say?' Gobshites cause a lot of upset to those around them. Ruining, forgetting, staining and smashing things is their speciality. They don't see these actions as wrong. If the event was ruined by their behaviour, everyone needs to lighten up. If they forgot, somebody should have reminded them. If they stained it, someone should have put a cover on it. If they smashed it, they were drunk and therefore innocent. Explaining to a gobshite why you're upset with them is a negative-energy vortex. The more you explain, the more annoyed you become. The more upset you become, the more the gobshite thinks your reaction is 'over the top'.

6) *At family functions, before the guests arrive, does someone pull them to one side and say, 'Don't you open your mouth this time!'?*

Have you seen others attempt to prepare this person for how they are expected to act in a social setting? Chances are this person is the kind of gobshite who has ruined family gatherings, first dates, client meetings, annual employee reviews, funerals and Christmases by saying things any normal person would regard as obviously inappropriate. 'I heard you got a vasectomy.' 'How much do you get paid before tax?' 'His last girlfriend was very different from you ... has he not mentioned her to you?' 'I was convinced you two were going to get engaged.' 'Your man Trump has made life a lot better for a lot of people.'

7) *Are they the reason special rules have been put in place?*

Owing to their ability to make problem-free things problematic, gobshites are often the cause of internal reviews, investigations and rule changes. Whether it's in the workplace, at your local pub or just around the family home, many, if not all, the newer rules were created because a gobshite pushed the limits. Just as a home with a toddler has spongy corners glued to the coffee table, organisations with gobshites have to future-proof themselves from their tendency to hurt themselves and others. 'We need a handrail there because of the incident with Sean last year.' 'Nobody is allowed near the compactor without written permission. We all know what happened to Mark last year.' 'Bottles are not allowed in the school since Brian choked on the cap last September.' 'They had to do that because your man Paul nearly burned his hand off.' It is estimated that companies across Ireland spend close to €500 million per year on gobshite-related safety training, equipment and protocol implementation.

8) *Are many people aware of this person for questionable reasons?*

'That's your man who broke both his legs jumping off the roof?' 'Did I see you with the fella who's always getting thrown out of Quinn's Bar?' 'Aren't you the lad who called in the bomb threat to the school and forgot to hide his number?' Gobshites always have a dubious track record, of which they are strangely proud. 'Two bomb threats actually!' Oftentimes they will see themselves as a hero or as a bit of a local celebrity. They readily confuse fame, infamy and notoriety. A gobshite thinks he has earned a level of renown in his village, while bar owners and the police would say he is notorious for his antics at the weekend. The gobshite can't see the difference between being well known and being named regularly in the local magistrate's court. When people stop, stare or point while giggling, these gobshites revel in the attention. 'Why are those people pointing and laughing at you, Paul?' 'It's all part of being a local legend. You get used to it.'

Gobshite Vernacular

A gobshite will never remain silent, even if they have nothing to say. It's a sad fact of life upon which the internet was built. Why say nothing when you can come out with these gems? 'The subtitles aren't on the screen long enough for me to read them. This movie is a load of bollocks.' 'Where are my keys, oh wait, hang on, they're in my pocket. I thought I had lost them there for a second but they were in the pocket where I normally keep them. That's mad. I fully thought they were gone. I hate losing things but I'm always losing things.'

Tuning out the white noise of a gobshite is a skill required in most jobs. However, in certain key moments, it is equally crucial to be able to tune in to and understand what a gobshite is saying. Here is a simple guide to help you distinguish their meaningless inner-monologue ramblings from red-flag-veiled admissions of guilt.

> *'There's something wrong with the handle on that door. It's stuck or something.'*

(Translation: I have broken the handle on the door.)

Gobshites will rarely take ownership of their mistakes even when shown CCTV footage of themselves pissing into the water supply. 'That might not be me!' Always assume that when a gobshite brings a broken item or issue to your attention, they are the cause of it. They will attempt to appear confused or concerned by the issue. 'I'm worried that dog might have a pain in his stomach' translates to 'I fed the dog something I shouldn't have and now I feel bad that the dog is clearly in pain. Please help and don't blame me.'

> *'I reckon there's a link between the rivers and the stars in the sky. I'm fairly sure they're connected.'*
>
> (Translation: I am really struggling to think of anything to say to you. Now I'm going to take a wild swing to see if maybe I can draw you into talking to me.)

These are the kinds of sentences that gobshites spout while you're trying to read or fill out crucial paperwork. Silence is an uncomfortable setting for all gobshites. They panic and assume that someone needs to say something. The above sentence is basically meaningless. It deserves no response, but that in itself can lead to further questions. 'I have you thinking now, don't I?' Distract the gobshite or bounce the ball back to them by saying, 'You should Google that and see if there's any research on it.' By weaponising their own laziness against them and assigning some form of work you can scare them away from the topic.

> *'How come nobody told me?'*
>
> (Translation: I didn't listen when I was being told something. Now I am blaming you for not spelling it out to me while holding me by the shoulders.)

Gobshites' inability to concentrate is matched only by their inability to open their fecking ears and listen to what is being said to them. Explaining something to a gobshite is like trying to dispose of whipped cream down the kitchen sink. You have to circle the drain and go round and round, again and again. It seems like it's going in but most of the time the real substance doesn't make it in there. Gobshites think that part of the process of following orders is returning to the person who gave the order to get more clarity. 'Which trash can did you say these go in?' When a gobshite wonders aloud, 'How come nobody told me?', they genuinely believe nobody gave them the information.

'You can't park there, pal.'

(Translation: I think I am hilarious.)

This phrase is typically said to someone who has been in a traffic accident. If their car is in an unusual position, in a bush, on the centre reservation or in a ditch, a gobshite driving past will slow down and inform the victim that they cannot park their car where it is. This is the height of gobshite comedy. Anyone that says this should have their driving licence revoked. Anyone who laughs at this has to seriously consider how they are encouraging gobshites and their obnoxious behaviour.

'It was like that when I got here.'

(Translation: Please don't blame me for breaking the item I have just broken.)

'It was like that when I got here' is among the most-used gobshite phrases because gobshites leave a trail of destruction behind them wherever they go. They break so many things so regularly that 'It was like that when I got here' is almost a reflex reaction to being accused of anything. Blocked toilets, soiled sheets, dog food in the fridge, it really doesn't matter how culpable they are for the event or situation they find themselves in. A gobshite will attempt to tell you they are innocent even if caught red-handed with chocolate all over their face.

'Why are people so uptight?'

(Translation: Why can't people allow me to say anything I like and live by my very low standards?)

If a person accuses you of being too uptight, no fun, or too focused on your work, marriage or remaining sober, recognise these assertions for what they are: massive telltale signs you might be dealing with a gobshite. Pointing out that a gobshite has done something wrong has never, ever worked out well. They rarely say, 'You have a point there. I really should not have tried to ride the dog like a horse even if I felt the dog was strong enough to carry me.' More often than not they will make your preference for health and safety, manners or time-keeping the issue.

'Why are you looking at me like that?'

(Translation: I have done something wrong / Will you fight me?)

There are two very different meanings to this phrase. One is antagonistic, while the other reveals that the gobshite has done something wrong. When a gobshite is guilty, which is very regularly, they will feel like everyone in the room is looking at them. If you get asked by a gobshite why you are looking at them a certain way, this gobshite either broke, stole or forgot something important; or they want to fight you. In the first instance you will need to press the gobshite on what they have done. This could take up to an hour. And in the second instance you need to leave the situation as soon as physically possible. In my old secondary school, gobshites would ask me to look at them: 'Hey, Regan, look at me. Look at me. Regan. Why aren't you looking at me? Regan, look at me. Here. Here. Here. Regan. Rego. Jarlath. Look at me for fuck sake.' I would then turn around to look at them and they would retort with, 'What the fuck are you looking at me for? I'll beat the head off you, Regan. Looking at me. Who do you think you are?' I've seen the same gobshite mind trick executed in other countries by much older gobshites. It never works out well.

'What time was I meant to be here?'

(Translation: I am late.)

Feigning ignorance is as cunning as a gobshite can get. Saying 'What day is it today?' on a birthday that has been talked about for months in advance is to a gobshite the equivalent of cracking the Enigma code. They might even discuss with you and others how clever they think it is to pretend not to know. 'I'll just say I didn't hear I needed one when I get asked by the police for my driving licence.' It's truly hilarious that gobshites who already fail to internalise directions, instructions, important safety protocols, names, dates and crucial financial rules think that leaning into their reputation as unreliable morons is the way to go when trouble arises. 'Sure, how would I know?' 'Why are you asking me?' 'Sure, I never get this stuff right' are their go-to lines when a gobshite definitely had the time and knowledge necessary to do something but didn't 'bother their bollocks'.

'Everybody calm down.'

(Translation: People are justifiably upset with me and I'd like that to stop now.)

Gobshites elicit anger from those who are calm 99 per cent of the time. A gobshite could make the most devout Buddhist monk scrunch up his chubby fists into balls and say the words 'Why are you such a pain in the hole?' It's their gift. If you want to get in touch with your anger, ask a gobshite to do something very basic for you. 'Everyone needs to calm down' is a phrase that a gobshite uses not knowing that saying this to those who are upset with them for good reason will only serve to upset them further. The gobshite may then remark, 'You see, this is what I'm talking about!'

Are There More Male Gobshites Than Female?

There are approximately eight male gobshites for every one female gobshite on the planet today. Anthropologists can't agree on why there is this gender imbalance in the population or why female gobshites are so head-melting in their behaviours. The world has grown accustomed to male gobshites, while female gobshites largely go forgotten due to their scarcity. You can find hundreds of male gobshites in the stands at a football game, thousands at a car show or tourist attraction, but finding two female gobshites together in one place is exceptionally hard. They are a rare solitary bird of prey that keeps flying into glass doors. CCTV footage from boyband reunion tours is usually the only source to show more than two female gobshites in the same location.

WHY ARE FEMALE GOBSHITES SO SCARCE?

Lady gobshites are not tolerated in the same way their male counterparts are. Mothers and fathers of male gobshites will tend to say, 'Go easy on Sean, he's only learning.' Even when Sean is in his late forties and has operated an electric lawn mower hundreds of times, he will be forgiven for mowing over the wire or destroying the grass. Female gobshites receive heavy criticism for locking themselves out of their house, putting plastic in toasters or asking recently bereaved widows, 'How is himself doing?' This early punishment seems to snap them out of the gobshite haze in their youth. So does that mean that a female gobshite is not a lost cause? Yes.

UNLIKE MALE GOBSHITES, FEMALE GOBSHITES ARE CAPABLE OF CHANGE

Young girls who display gobshite characteristics early in life, such as failing to see the imminent danger posed by putting their fingers into electrical sockets, can straighten up and fly right in a short period of time. The female gobshite seems to be capable of learning while the male is almost always a lost cause from day one. Sarah might have gone on an inter-railing trip at 17 where she lost her wallet, and cost her family a small fortune in unpaid parking tickets but now she works for Bank of Ireland in Ashbourne. Your cousin Frank, by contrast, has been falling for scam emails for the last 10 years with no signs of this behaviour changing any time soon.

THIS IS A MALE GOBSHITE'S WORLD

It's a sad fact that the patriarchal patterns of modern society mean that men are at an advantage to women in the workplace. They get better jobs. They get more jobs. They get better-paid jobs than their female counterparts. Depressingly, the same is true for male gobshites. A male gobshite enjoys a vastly higher number of career progression opportunities than a female gobshite. While a male gobshite can rise undetected through a series of failed business ventures, bankruptcies and criminal investigations to the office of President of the United States of America, a female gobshite will struggle to hold an office administrator job for any length of time.

This gross discrepancy seems to work to screen out female gobshites or force them to raise their game, learn from their mistakes and change. Much of the world simply won't allow female gobshites to exist unchecked, while many thundering male gobshites are held up as icons of style (Kanye West), innovators (Elon Musk) and heroes (Tiger Woods).

There are exceptions to the rule, of course. Certain dogged and resilient female gobshites survive and thrive in our male-dominated world. The hospitality and airline industries attract and actively promote a system of positive discrimination towards the hiring of complete and utter gobshites, whether they are male or female. Next time you are late and standing in line waiting for a clerk in a hotel or check-in desk to finish texting or chatting with their friends, remember the company you are trying to do business with is doing its part in encouraging gobshites to keep being gobshites.

ARE FEMALE GOBSHITES ATTRACTED TO MALE GOBSHITES?

For the most part, yes. Female gobshites tend to pair off with male gobshites because they fail to see the flaws that the rest of the world can't tolerate. Gobshites who are constantly late, who refuse to wear a watch or replace the smashed screen on their phone, or who don't allow themselves adequate time to get to where they need to go, can find love with someone similarly shambolic. 'That pair of gobshites deserve each other' is what those attending gobshite weddings will say. When two gobshites marry there is chaos ahead. The sight of the blind leading the blind over the cliff edge of starting a gobshite family is terrifying. Sadly, there is nothing governments can do about it.

DO FEMALE GOBSHITES MAKE
GOOD MOTHERS?

This might be the dumbest question ever committed to print. Female gobshites make terrible mothers. They can barely book a flight yet somehow now they are going to miraculously know how to raise another human being? In the best case scenario, when a female gobshite has a baby, the child becomes everyone else's problem. Gobshite parents created the phrase, 'It takes a village to raise a child'. Of course it fucking does when you're as clueless as the infant.

Anyone who has been unfortunate enough to have had a gobshite for a mother and survived to tell the tale is an impressive individual. In job interviews we should accept 'Had a gobshite parent' as a qualification. The person who manages to become a fully functioning adult having had a gobshite father or mother is built from something special. They have more than likely had to find a way to feed, entertain and educate themselves from day one. Pressure makes diamonds. Gobshite parents don't produce good human beings. They lose their kids on trips to the beach. The point is, if you have survived being raised by someone who sees you as an inconvenience, as an 18-year pain in the arse or someone else's problem – you are a diamond.

SPOTTING FEMALE GOBSHITES

Identifying lady gobshites in the world is trickier than spotting their male counterparts. Why? Because as we explained earlier – Jesus, have you been listening at all? – the female gobshite has been forced to assimilate to society in a way the male gobshite does not feel he has to. While a male gobshite will say, 'How was I supposed to know she wasn't pregnant? Look at the size of her belly' to the irate boyfriend of a woman he just insulted, a female gobshite is forced to play her cards much closer to her chest.

Female gobshites will tend to nod along to instructions they don't understand, whereas a male gobshite will stop the presentation and demand more clarity on something that is abundantly clear already. In this way the female gobshite can be more dangerous. She will sit the ice cream machine safety course, allow herself to be lectured for an hour on the dangers of using gone-off ice cream mix, literally hear nothing for the hour, just sit there thinking of how much she likes ice cream. She may then head back to work and give every customer for the next week salmonella because, yet again, she failed to clean the machine. You might ask, which is worse? The male gobshite who slowed down the safety presentation, asked to have the entire course explained more than three times, asked the dumbest questions and still went out and nearly lost his hand in the machine when trying to retrieve a cone from its inner workings – or the female gobshite who sent a few hundred people to the hospital and now thinks everyone is 'being very hard on her'.

One thing is for sure: male and female gobshites present their own unique challenges. No two gobshites are the same just as no two car crashes are the same. Sorting through the wreckage that gobshites leave behind, attempting to puzzle out what went wrong and why is as mind-numbing and never-ending a task as trying to explain how to safely use an ice cream machine.

'I JUST KEEP IT REAL!'

'I'm not going to apologise for that. I'm just being real.' Many female gobshites are obnoxious, abrupt and rude. They justify this behaviour by describing themselves as honest or 'too much for some people'. They might even tell you that upsetting people is a just a by-product of being as real as they are. They may tell you everyone but them is fake. It's important to understand that for this kind of gobshite, fake is a catch-all term for manners, discretion, empathy, subtitling and any form of quiet understanding. 'Real gobshites', as I like to refer to them, think that saying the unsayable is a mark of their courage rather than a sign of their ignorance. 'What did I say that was so wrong?' is their go-to sentence in these situations. In a later chapter we will look at the peculiar relationship that gobshites have with the truth.

'EVERYBODY IS BEING SO UNKIND TO ME!'

The victim complex of the female gobshite is perhaps the biggest giveaway of their existence. Lady gobshites will, when challenged on stupid things they have done, react as if they are being bullied by the person simply asking if they did the stupid thing.

'Did you put your red dress in with that whites wash?'

Lady gobshite: 'Why are you being so aggressive?' (almost in tears).

'You've ruined every white towel in the house, you gobshite!'

Lady gobshite: 'Why are you singling me out? Yes, I was the one that put the red dress in the wash with whites but you're acting like this is all my fault and I'm a horrible person' (now sobbing).

In this way female gobshites are extremely hard to reach, especially when they screw up important things.

ARE KARENS GOBSHITES? OR DID GOBSHITES CREATE KARENS?

It is incorrect to say that 'Not all female gobshites are Karens but all Karens are gobshites.' In the last 10 years the rise of the gobshite has coincided with the rise of the irate, unreasonable, loud and obnoxious female pest known as a 'Karen'. These women have been made famous through social media platforms and infamous through their choices of things to get mad at. The modern Karen has a hair-trigger temper and is prone to violence in a way that gobshites are not. This is a central and key difference between gobshites and Karens. Were these women this angry before they encountered a gobshite or did the gobshite husbands, sons, daughters and co-workers awaken the Karen within? Were Karens just normal women who overdosed on gobshites?

Which Came First – the Gobshite or the Karen?

It's safe to say that the gobshite arrived before the Karen. When we see a Karen in the wild we have to ask how many gobshites has this poor woman had to deal with if she is getting so unnecessarily angry over something as innocuous as a bin being left on a road. As discussed, gobshites have a capacity to draw anger from previously placid people. This skill, if you can call it that, is uncanny. If there is anger within you, a gobshite can find a way to trigger it. So perhaps the next Karen you meet might just need a hug. Definitely don't suggest this to her.

10

Sporting Gobshites

TIGER WOODS – GOLFER AND GOBSHITE

How can one of the most successful sports people the world has ever seen be a gobshite? When he decides that millions of dollars, a beautiful wife and kids, multiple mansions, cars and the respect of the world isn't enough. In what even he must now see as a gobshite move for the ages, he decided to sleep with multiple women while married to his long-suffering wife. Just like all true-blue, high-grade gobshites, he didn't seem to grasp that he would be caught. His subsequent fall from grace, ham-fisted apology and financial losses ($750 million divorce settlement and stock losses of $12 billion) were eye-watering. Even the biggest Tiger fans recognise this gobshite phase as being at a world-beating level. But there's more. While at the top of his game, before all the cheating, Tiger became obsessed with the Navy Seals. He forced himself to complete their training routine one summer and, in so doing, fucked up his back so badly that doctors feared he might never play golf the same way again. Sources close to the Woods medical team revealed years later that they all thought he was a danger to himself – a gobshite with a lot of money.

ALI DIA – FOOTBALLER AND GOBSHITE

In 1996, Southampton Football Club signed a gobshite by the name of Ali Dia who claimed to be a cousin of the Liberian star George Weah. Ali had virtually no top-flight football experience outside of playing FIFA on his Playstation, and even less of a connection to George Weah. Ali is a legendary sporting gobshite because his plan to play Premier League football actually worked for 53 minutes. Just in the door at the club, Ali was brought on as a substitute in an actual competitive league match. The appearance went so badly he was subbed off and released from his contract after just 14 days. Gobshites are often asked, 'What did you think was going to happen?' In true gobshite style, Ali Dia had not thought that far down the road. Like so many gobshites, Ali has somehow managed to do quite well in life. In 2001 he graduated with a business degree from Northumbria University. He received an MBA from San Francisco State University in 2003. He is now a successful businessman in Qatar – but can we really trust our information? It's a perplexing story and there is more than one gobshite in the tale of Ali Dia. Who was the gobshite manager that signed him to Southampton?

GRAEME SOUNESS – FOOTBALL MANAGER AND GOBSHITE

In the eyes of Liverpool fans, there is no greater gobshite in football than Graeme Souness. In 1991 this gobshite was somehow given the reins of a club that had dominated English football for decades. He immediately set about doing what gobshites do best: making a complete and utter balls of the entire situation, pissing everyone off and acting like none of it was his fault. Graeme falls into the category of gobshite who believes himself to be an unappreciated genius. He thought he was ahead of his time and would regularly tell the players that he was better than Bill Shankly (the club's most decorated and successful manager). Souness took the club from the top of the league to struggling to hold on to sixth place. Remarkable hubris and gobshitery were the hallmarks of his management style. Greame was the kind of sporting gobshite who thought every decision he made was the right one simply because he made it. Later moving to Southampton, was it any wonder he would be caught out by a genius like Ali Dia?

THE ULTIMATE WARRIOR AKA JAMES HELLWIG – WRESTLER AND GOBSHITE

In the golden era of WWF, when wrestling was among the most-watched sports in the world, when emergency rooms were full of kids who had power-slammed each other off couches, The Ultimate Warrior was a god. With his war paint, wild hair, bronzed skin and impossibly ripped body, Warrior was a fan favourite who drew energy from the crowd. He was a champion, an icon of the sport, known throughout the world, and all the while a horrible little gobshite of a man. According to his wrestling colleagues, he was the guy who refused to do the job right no matter how much trouble he got himself into. In doing so he created more work for everyone, just like your standard office gobshite. When the work is wrestling and not filing, that's a massive pain in the hole for everyone. He found problems where there were no problems. He got into feuds with other wrestlers over things there was no need to argue over. He was so rude to children who wanted his autograph that the WWF forced him to record an apology to the fans. Eventually he was suspended from the WWF for experimenting with human growth hormone. In 1993, Hellwig legally changed his name to Warrior. In spite of all this, people still liked James Hellwig and The Ultimate Warrior. Proof, if proof was needed, that gobshites sometimes have a lovable quality that defies logic.

Gobshites vs the Truth

'Is that true?'

'Yeah, no, yeah, I mean yeah, I think it is … I mean that's what I've heard.'

'It either is true or it isn't true. Did the manager say you could take home any food that wasn't eaten at the end of the day?'

'I mean like, I got it from the kitchen.'

'That's not what I asked.'

'What?'

'Did you have permission to bring home food from the restaurant?'

'Which … the food? It was left over.'

'I know it was left over but did you get the express permission from the manager to take it home?'

'The express? I don't know why you're getting so upset over this … I work there.'

At best, gobshites have a strained relationship with the truth and truthfulness. For some reason, gobshites believe that telling lies, half lies and bending the truth to accommodate what they are doing or have done is just how the world works. In previous chapters we have looked at how to spot a gobshite in the wild. Their relationship with honesty and the truth might be the biggest dead giveaway. The above dialogue captures some of the frustration this can cause. Instead of admitting the jig is up, the gobshite who knows he is caught will defend his position to the very end, try to muddy the waters and obfuscate responsibility. 'I don't know, I'm fairly sure I saw other lads doing it!'

LIES, DAMN LIES AND DUMB LIES

Gobshites tell lies even when lies aren't needed. It's like a tic. Even when they are not in trouble, a gobshite will add extra half truths on top of existing tales in the hope that it ingratiates them with the group. 'Oh yeah, sure I know all them lads. I can get in there for free any time I like.' In this instance, a gobshite is pretending to know how to get into a nightclub. He does not know any of 'them lads'. In fact, 'them lads' may have even thrown him out of the nightclub recently. For many gobshites, this is enough to be able to say they have a pre-existing relationship. You and I would not say we know a police officer who gave us a speeding ticket. A gobshite might say, 'Don't worry about anything, lads, I know the cops around here really well. They think I'm sound.'

A lot of the gobshite's lies can be explained by examining this kind of warped view of reality. A regular person can have the same experience as a gobshite but their description of the incident would be completely different. Let's look at an example.

Imagine a woman was to end a relationship with a man after a couple of months by saying, 'I don't think it's working out. I feel like I got into the relationship a bit too soon. You're a really nice person and I've had a lot of fun with you but I really need to get my career in order before I can give any relationship the time it deserves.'

The regular man would understand and tell his friends, 'Ah, what can you do, she was really nice, we got on well but the timing wasn't right. She was really straight with me and I respected her for that. It's a shame because I think at a different time in our lives, it could have worked out, but who knows.'

The gobshite, by contrast, would tell his friends, 'She was mental. She started spouting on some shite about the universe and the planets aligning or something. I drifted off while she was talking. She was like it was "too soon". Too soon after what, like? I actually think she was mad in the head and absolutely obsessed with her work. I don't really know what she did for a living but she's like, "I'm just going to focus on my work." I mean come on, are you not going to drink pints at all? I hate when women lie to ya. Just come out and say it – you don't think you're good enough for me.'

A GOBSHITE'S VIEW OF THE WORLD

The gobshite's perception of what is actually happening before them cannot be relied upon; this is an important point to understand. They make terrible witnesses in court and even worse referees. All of our interpretations of the world are cut with our own personal experience, opinion and confirmation bias. With a gobshite, the connection to objective truth is completely skewed after years of difficult experiences (being blamed for things going wrong), unfounded opinions based on their own ineptitude (bulbs never screw in, they always break in your hand) and biases formed as a result of their inability to move through the world smoothly (it's impossible to save money nowadays because you always have to pay fines for things).

As a direct result of this, it's startling to see how simple things that are obvious to the rest of us can be viewed completely differently by a gobshite. Here are a few examples of things any normal person can observe in the world versus how a gobshite sees them.

A personal trainer advises you to hydrate well before training and to make sure to stretch after your session. They make a joke about how you have come a long way from where you started and encourage you to stay positive.

A normal person:
'The PT is sound. He gives me a lot of common-sense advice that I'm inclined to forget. He has a sense of humour and I feel like he is proud of the progress I have made. I get the sense that he knows I struggle with negative self talk and that if I can get on top of that, everything will just click.'

A gobshite:
'Your man the PT lad is melting my head. The other day he started to take the piss out of me at the end of the session. Ehh, we don't know each other that well, for fuck's sake. I'm fairly sure he's either obsessed with me or he fancies me. One or the other. Some of the shite he comes out with. He has to be thinking, this lad is in better shape than me. I could be a PT if I wanted to be, ya know?'

Notice how the gobshite didn't hear the most basic advice around drinking water and stretching. The ego of many gobshites is so large they assume that any kindness constitutes a romantic advance or is proof that a person is 'obsessed with me'.

After servicing your car, the mechanic recommends you consider replacing the water tank. He says the car is running well considering the natural wear and tear you have put on it over the last few years of driving, but the cracks he has noticed in the water tank will only get worse. He did everything he could to patch them up for now but next time it might be worthwhile changing the tank completely. He changed the front tyres but said the back ones seemed okay and he threw in a free valet.

A normal person:
'Getting my car serviced is always a stress. I'm always terrified that the bill is going to be huge. I don't really know much about cars so there is a lot of trust involved. Thankfully my mechanic is really straight with me and never seems to charge over the odds. Like today, he could have said I needed four new tyres and a water tank. Now at least I know what's coming on the next service and I can budget for that.'

A gobshite:
'I'm fairly sure that mechanic I'm going to is a con artist. Water tank leak? Have you ever in all your life? Cars don't have water tanks, they have fuel tanks. I'm looking at him while he's lying through his teeth thinking, "You must think I'm thick as two short planks!" Then he's like, oh, the back tyres are fine and the front tyres aren't. How? Like how the fuck would that be the case? I'm not driving around on two wheels. He's all like, next time … I was like, there won't be a next time, pal. It ended in a big row anyway and I refused to pay him. I paid in the end but he was shitting himself.'

Your sister calls to say that your parents need help cleaning out their shed this weekend. They are hoping to get rid of some of the old boxes of your childhood stuff that they have been holding there for you. Would you be free to come back at some point to help? Your father recently had a hip replacement.

A normal person:
'I had to change my plans for the weekend because my parents need me to sort out some stuff back at their place. They've been holding on to a lot of my precious things from when I was at school. It's a pain in the arse but it's going to be amazing to have all this stuff at my place now.'

A gobshite:
'My sister blocked me out of it on the phone this morning for leaving stuff at our parents' house. Eh, where the hell else am I going to leave it? Apparently they are doing some sort of spring clean or some shit. This is all my mother and her OCD. Why the fuck do they need to clean out the shed anyway? Like, what's the panic? I'm not changing my plans. I mean I'm not doing anything this weekend but I might be going out on Saturday so Sunday will be a write-off.'

(Note: the gobshite feels victimised right away.)

There's been an accident at work!

A normal person:
'I hope everyone is okay. What happened?'

A gobshite:
'I suppose I'm going to be blamed for this too.'

The child has lost his teddy bear. Your partner says you need to drive back and check if it's in the hotel.

A normal person:
'Ahh no. Well I suppose if it's our only option, that's what we will have to do. Is the child very upset?'

A gobshite:
'For fuck's sake, it's just a teddy. This is bullshit.'

The police have told you to get your tail light fixed. They let you off with a warning this time.

A normal person:
'I got lucky there. I'll put a reminder in my phone to get that done this week. A different police officer would have given me a fine on the spot.'

A gobshite:
'That's proof they can't fine you for these stupid things. I will in my bollix get it fixed. If another policeman stops me I'll just give him the same line I gave this one. I'm going to sell this car eventually. I'm not wasting money on improving it now.'

SPOTTING A GOBSHITE IN A WHATSAPP GROUP CHAT

We've all found ourselves in multiple Whatsapp group chats making suggestions, exchanging gifs and making plans with faceless people we might never ordinarily befriend. Being able to identify the gobshites in this environment is a crucial modern life skill. It is vital that we remain vigilant while engaging in these fun back and forth chats. There's nothing a modern gobshite likes more than using the cover of a WhatsApp group to explain away the shitstorm they have created. 'But sure didn't I say it in the WhatsApp group?' is a gobshite get-out-of-jail card that could implicate you by association. Remember, to avoid drowning in full responsibility, a gobshite clings to any piece of wood that floats by.

Can you spot the gobshite in these WhatsApp conversations? Hint: There may be more than one.

Sean:
What time is the match on today?

Brian:
I'm fairly sure it's 3

                                                        Trev
                                                          3

Martin
FFS 3 ya dope.

Sean
3PM?

Keith
No 3am - I swear you get thicker by the day lad.

Sean
Cool. Do we need to bring the kit back from the last match?

Brian

Yeah. Mick went mental the last time coz only four lads brought the kit and two of them hadn't bothered their hole to wash it.

Sean

Were we meant to watch it.

Was it

Wash it

Fucking autocorrect is such a pain in the whole.

Trev

Don't bring it back if you haven't washed it.

Sean

Oh fuck. Should I try to wash it now?

Martin

No you should try to buy and identical kit off one off the internet. Clown. 😂😂

Mike

😂😂😂😂

Brian

PMSL 😂😂

Martin

😂😂 You're some dope. If it isn't that smelly you'll probably get away with it.

Sean

Sound.

Keith
Lads, ye know Mick is in this WhatsApp group. Ye better delete those messages fast.

Sean
Oh fuck!

Brian
Why didn't ye tell me yiz absolutely bastards.

Mick
Lads the kits are needed for the junior B match. I'm not being a hard ass when I ask ye to wash them and the return them. It's just manners.

Sean
Sorry Mick.

(30 mins later) Haha! I was only messing Mick.

Answer: Sean and Brian are gobshites. Neither of them took the time to check if their coach Mick was in the team WhatsApp group. When notified of this, rather than deleting their messages they chose to text the replies 'oh fuck' and 'Why didn't ye tell me yiz absolutely bastards'. The later reply removes any doubt over Sean's gobshite status. Rather than falling on his sword and admitting his wrongdoing or quickly fixing it, he chooses to blame others for not informing him of obvious information freely available to all. The ham-fisted attempts to shrug off the interaction as harmless fun is textbook gobshite behaviour. In the future, Sean and Brian will run punishment laps at training on Tuesday evening. When they fail to wash and return their kits the following week they will be informed that their punishment laps will double each time they commit the infringement. Sean and Brian will then drop off the team, preferring to tell everyone in the local pub and their parents that coach Mick was 'out to get them'.

12

Gobshites in Relationships

The heart wants what the heart wants. And sometimes the heart is stupid. Gobshites confound expectations. They are unemployable, yet they consistently find well-paying important jobs. They are un-bringable fucking anywhere, yet they show up to everything. They are completely undateable, and yet they find love.

A GOBSHITE IN SHEEP'S CLOTHING – HOW GOBSHITES DISGUISE THEMSELVES TO LURE YOU IN

'He seems nice.'

It is crucial to know that not all gobshites present as gobshites on day one of a relationship. On a first date, a drink with friends, or a chance encounter, a gobshite's true identity may not be immediately uncovered. Short interactions work better with gobshites, simply because their head-melting ways require more time to be understood. What appears quirky and fun in a brief conversation could cost you your sanity over the course of six months.

Many unfortunate women only learn their husband is a gobshite after they are married. For many, a honeymoon turns out to be a gobshite reveal party, where instead of finding out if you need to buy girls' clothes or boys' clothes, you find out your life is going to be a nightmare. Going away together is the acid test of whether or not the person you fancy is a gobshite.

Why does it take so long to know if some people are gobshites? Because gobshites can be a lot of fun. Their freewheeling attitude to the details of life can even be attractive. 'He's just so fun. He's not all serious like my last boyfriend. He just lives in the moment' is a glowing review regularly given to complete gobshites after a first date. This man might be incapable of paying a phone bill, washing himself properly or anticipating that you might like a gift for Valentine's Day, but over a few drinks he makes you laugh.

GOBSHITES DON'T DO COMMITMENT WELL

For gobshites, committing to doing things is a problem – whether it's being at a certain place at a certain time or just brushing their teeth. True gobshites struggle to stick to plans. This makes romantic involvement a minefield. What is a romantic relationship other than a set of commitments? What's romantic about them is that nobody has to articulate the commitments, and therein lies the problem for the gobshite. If it is not spelled out to them, they will struggle to do a thing. Even when something *is* spelled out to them, they struggle to do it. Most gobshites don't have car insurance for this very reason. 'Nobody told me I needed car insurance!' they will protest. A judge or officer of the law eventually tells them they need car insurance, then they fail to get car insurance because 'nobody ever told me where to get car insurance!' This type of thinking is relationship kryptonite and gobshites have a mine full to the brim with the stuff.

'SHE WAS SO DEMANDING! SHE KEPT TELLING ME WHERE I NEEDED TO BE'

Gobshites regularly fail in the relationship setting because, as we'll see in the employment chapter, the most basic assumptions regarding their role seem strange and outlandish to them. If a gobshite's girlfriend reminds him they have a dinner reservation, he will view this as her trying to 'control' him. Plans, responsibilities and arrangements of any sort are problematic for most gobshites, which puts their partner in the awkward position of having to remind them constantly of what is expected of them. This drains the relationship of any sort of romance and the partner of the will to live. We often see the girlfriend becoming less of the gobshite boyfriend's life partner and more their carer.

'HE'S AN AWFUL GOBSHITE BUT HE'S IMPROVING'

Many women, while acknowledging that their partner is without doubt a fully fledged gobshite, take the approach of working on him like an old broken-down car. In time he will run well. In cases like this, the woman concerned sees her boyfriend as a project. With enough tinkering and encouragement, she thinks she can work out the kinks in his personality. This is dangerous thinking. Being a gobshite isn't a kink in a personality any more than being a serial killer is a quirk in a person's character. A person who thinks they can pester, coax or badger a gobshite out of being a gobshite is signing up for a lifetime of misery.

On the surface it seems possible to change gobshites and their behaviour. It's not unreasonable to imagine you could get a person who keeps locking themselves out of their house to start remembering to bring their keys. It sounds feasible, on the surface, the idea of teaching a person how to avoid burning their fingers by waiting until the toast has popped before attempting to retrieve it from the toaster. But gobshites are not like other people. Someone who keeps locking himself out of his house might be aided by a keychain attached to his trousers, or a spare key in case of emergencies. But a true gobshite will find a way of losing the keychain and spare key. You might help a normal person who keeps burning their hands on a toaster by telling them that it is possible to turn the toaster off at the wall and allow it to cool down. A certified gobshite will nod at you while you are saying these things only to later use a knife on the live toaster.

The path to a happy romantic life is littered with the bodies of women who believed they could convert a gobshite. You are not John the Baptist. Gobshites are not just people with strange beliefs who will see the light when you show it to them. They will try to turn the light off or break the switch. Millions of women each year devote time to convincing their friends that their man is on the verge of being converted from gobshite into a fully functioning, non-burping, romantic plan-making, birthday card-buying human being. Bickering elderly couples are not just cranky old people: for the most part they comprise a completely exhausted woman who believed she could change her gobshite husband into a normal person and a gobshite man so steadfast in his gobshite ways that he is willing to fight over the smallest things. Do your elderly parents argue in public over absolute nonsense? You might need to come to terms with the possibility that they are not mentally declining. You might need to sit down, take a few deep breaths and consider the possibility that your father is a gobshite and your mother is the idealist who thought she could fix him.

In a perfect world, all women would receive gobshite identification training at secondary school. Gobshites in government have stopped attempts to bring in such training programmes because they fear that they might lose their jobs, not to mention the damage it would do to the economy. Think about how much money you would save if you could identify a gobshite electrician on sight. The rise in online booking and dating apps has given a new lease of life to gobshite tradespeople, taxi drivers, restaurant owners and prospective boyfriends across the globe.

SWIPE RIGHT – GOBSHITES LOVE DATING APPS

In recent times, dating apps have given gobshites the opportunity to con unsuspecting women into dating them. Gobshites have been going on more dates than ever before. For all its faults, the face-to-face screening process in the past allowed for the female gobshite radar to operate. Just as telltale signs can be observed during an in-person meeting with a gobshite posing as a regular person, red flags can also be found in the profiles of gobshites on dating websites and apps.

Here are some red flags in dating profile pics. Put a little tick next to each one you have seen.

Flexing muscles: Doing the 'I'm a big strong boy' pose of any sort should be enough to make a person swipe by a prospective romantic partner. Flexing muscles is like putting a gobshite arrow above your head. It removes all doubt.

☐ Kissy face: Similar to the flex, the kissy face is a statement of intent and content. This person wants physical contact rather than emotional connection. With all the facial expressions available, kissy face is at the bottom of the ladder and should set off alarm bells.

☐ Fist under chin looking into the middle distance: Gobshites who do this pose in their profile photo want you to believe that they are thoughtful. They've seen people thinking but they've never tried it themselves. The person who puts their fist under their chin and gazes wistfully into the horizon is dangerously shallow and could be a serial killer.

☐ Cap on sideways, sunglasses or tongue out: A gobshite who wears any of these things or does a combination of these things is trying to tell you, 'I'm fun'. In reality, they are the opposite of that.

☐ Yoga pose: This gobshite thinks that sitting cross-legged makes him a more thoughtful person. He thinks you're stupid. He is trying to lure you into engaging with him on a subject he knows nothing about. Mindfulness is to gobshites what bicycles are to fish. A gobshite doing a sun salutation in their profile photo is using something you might like as a substitute for a personality. Many people start dating people who also happen to like yoga. The gobshite who puts it in his profile pic is either so obsessed with yoga he has nothing else going on in his life, or he has heard from a gobshite friend that this is a great way to avoid 'fat birds'. Avoid at all costs.

☐ Puppy in profile pic: Exploiting an animal to distract from a gobshite's lack of discernible qualities might appear smart on the surface, but chances are this is not the gobshite's dog. Beware of any gobshite who claims to have had a pet in the past. Taking care of anyone, even a pet, is a problem for all gobshites. It poses such a huge challenge to them that it leaves them with no energy left to spare. A romantic relationship with a gobshite with a pet will work out worse for you than any of the puppies, fish or cats he has lost over the years.

ROMANTIC GESTURES

Unsurprisingly, the concept of romance is entirely lost on gobshites. Attempting to explain it to them is as pointless an endeavour as trying to teach a toaster to boil water. The part of a gobshite's brain that deals with romance and gestures that could be viewed as romantic is not plugged in at the wall. They don't even hear the phone ring when the opportunity to do something romantic presents itself. But that is not to say they will not attempt to be romantic.

Many gobshites in relationships will be forced to 'do something romantic' after an argument or bust-up. Gobshites save a lot of money on flowers as a result of only buying them after Valentine's Day. Think of the gobshite's romantic impulses as a faulty smoke alarm. There's something there but it serves no practical purpose. The gobshite will only attempt to do a romantic thing when the house is ablaze. Rather than detecting the need for romance in the weeks leading up to the anniversary or relationship milestone, they wait until the emergency is upon them. The gobshite's romantic endeavours come from a place of panic rather than kind, gentle, empathetic, loving thoughtfulness. Consequently, if you see a gobshite with flowers, they are usually running as fast as they can. For a gobshite, any romantic gesture they might come up with can typically be categorised as an attempt to throw water on the flames of a burning relationship, rather than feathers to line their nest. They think flowers are to be thrust at a woman with folded arms, rather than gently placed in a vase on their bedside table. It's a known fact that gobshites are unaware that flowers require water.

Romance is the equivalent of a frequency of sound that gobshites cannot hear. They are oblivious to the deafening blast of suggestions that surround them in the lead-up to Valentine's Day, in the same way dogs can't hear the lyrics of Taylor Swift's music. Just as you can play 'Shake It Off' all day to a spaniel, he's never going to sing it. You can take a gobshite to the window of a jeweller's and tell them directly to their face the rings you would like to receive as a gift, but it will never occur to the gobshite that this is a pointed hint. That is not to say that gobshites don't buy rings. The gobshite ring business is booming. Jewellers know that gobshites panic-buying rings that are long overdue gives them their biggest opportunity to turn a profit. It is estimated that 75 per cent of profit margins across the global diamond industry can be traced to gobshites attempting to make up for shit they either should have done some time ago or relationship milestones they claim 'nobody reminded me about'.

Here's how to spot a gobshite's romantic gesture.

Lack of Thought

'I rang and asked you if you wanted flowers … what?' Gobshites think a romantic gesture such as giving flowers is just another item on a shopping list. Eggs, milk, flowers. That's how their brain works. It's very common for a gobshite to ask the person they are in a relationship with if they would like something romantic to be done for them. Their brain cannot comprehend the idea that asking if you would like something romantic undoes the potential for romance. You can explain this to them if you like but be prepared for the following sentence: 'How am I supposed to know when you'd like something romantic? There's absolutely no winning with you.'

Timing

Whether it's asking a recently bereaved person why they're so sad or jostling an elderly relative to surprise them in the street, timing is always an issue with a gobshite. Aside from their gross stupidity, the gobshite's inability to correctly 'read the room' – to understand any nuance or mood in a particular situation – could constitute their most significant limitation. If you are to receive a romantic gesture from a gobshite you are dating, the easiest identifying characteristic will be the poor timing of the gesture. It will either be way too late or will occur at a moment that isn't appropriate. Too late is the most obvious of the two options here. Ninety-nine per cent of gobshite birthday gifts are presented the day after the birthday itself. The other one per cent are bought at a filling station, and are presented in the late evening with the price still on by the still-panting-and-covered-with-sweat gobshite. Has a love interest of yours ever presented you with something intimate in front of other family members? Bingo. He's a gobshite. It lines up with their poor impulse control. The gobshite has a thing for you, you are here, so here it is.

The Gift/Gesture Itself

Gobshite gifts/gestures are never what you asked for, suggested or hinted at. Even when you send them a photo, a link and a shop address. Even when you transfer the money to their account so that they can afford the thing you said you'd like for your anniversary so that we don't have a repeat of last year, a gobshite will find a way to fuck it up.

You ask for flowers but not lilies. The gobshite will produce a bunch of lilies. 'I couldn't remember if you said no lilies or nothing but lilies will do. I'll run down and change them.' Two hours later: 'I fell on the way back to the florist's. Can you bring me to A&E?'

You have sensitive skin. He knows this. He watches you each night taking extra special care to be kind to your skin and not aggravate it. You only use gentle soaps and creams. He has been surrounded by them for more than two years. The gobshite gets you a tube of facial scrub, 'coz you're always rubbing that muck into your face. How is this not what you wanted? I even checked, it's in a white tube like the ones you already use for fuck's sake. You're impossible, you know that. I'm not allowed be romantic.'

The Blame

Rest assured your gobshite will get it wrong. And when he does, in his opinion the responsibility for his failure will lie at your door. Just as when a gobshite causes an accident at work because 'nobody warned me', they are also convinced that any failure to achieve a sufficient level of romance is down to you and your insane standards. Watch out for this victim blaming. The gobshite is a master at convincing those around them that if they had taken better care of them, none of this would have happened. Relationships are no different. 'You said you wanted a holiday. I'm bringing you on holiday with me and the lads and still that's not good enough!' When a gobshite is accused of not making enough effort they will explain the level of effort involved in them being thoughtless. 'Do you have any idea how long it took me to find a place that would engrave your name onto that shield? That shield is very important to me. You know I love that shield. I won it in a raffle for fuck's sake.'

WHAT SHOULD I DO IF I THINK I MIGHT BE DATING A GOBSHITE?

1) *Run.* If you've read this book and are now fully sure this person is a gobshite, then the first option is to get the hell out of the building. Don't delay. The longer you tether yourself to a gobshite, the harder it becomes to get out the toilet window. Make your excuses and leave as fast as your legs will carry you. Leave no chink of light. You need to make it abundantly clear that the relationship is over. Many people have had to break up with gobshites multiple times before the gobshite internalises what is happening. 'I thought you were only messing', 'What? People say I never want to see you again all the time, I just thought you were mad at me.' Think of delivering the break-up news as trying to remove glitter. You're going to need to scrub harder than you've ever scrubbed to get rid of this gobshite. And even then, like glitter, he will keep appearing for months, maybe even years, to come.

2) *Consult your friends.* If you're not entirely sure whether or not this person is a full-blown gobshite, ask those closest to you for their opinion. If this person is a gobshite your friends and family will be dying for you to ask. They may have been biting their fists every time the gobshite leaves the room. They may have been making 'shoot myself in the head' gestures to each other while the gobshite has been talking. Having said that, while those closest to you will have an opinion, they might be reluctant to give it. They

may say, 'Why do you ask?' or 'I don't know, he's a very eccentric character.' Push them on any vagueness. You need to know. If the person you're dating is a gobshite, this will be an open door to push. Once you have confirmation – 'Hand on heart, he's a complete gobshite, you can do so much better, none of us can understand why you're dating him' – refer to option one. RUN!

3) *Don't kid yourself.* Many people have wasted years convinced that they can change an unromantic, gormless gobshite into a Ryan Gosling in *The Notebook*. They think they can carve him down or mould his complete lack of manners and tact into something that won't make everyone roll their eyes or cancel their plans to meet up with you when they find out 'he's coming too.' It's not going to happen. Gobshites are almost reptilian in their ability to adapt to change. If you cut off the part of him that keeps running up credit card debt, two new tentacles will grow in its place. A gobshite will find a way to be a gobshite with whatever material you give him. Telling yourself you can change a gobshite makes you look like a gobshite. These people are the reason the term 'ignorance is bliss' was coined. They are at their happiest when they at their most oblivious. Thinking you can change a gobshite into an evolved, empathetic, considerate lover is like thinking you can convince a cat to bark. Even if the cat barks, it won't know what it's doing. So what's the point?

13

Gobshites and Their Mothers

'Look at this gobshite. I'd say his mother is proud of him!' In a lot of cases, yes, gobshites' mothers are proud of them. Why? Because mothers of gobshites are the main reason they exist. Sure, many people are born with gobshite DNA or a heritage of generational gobshitery that they cannot avoid, but most are just people who never got a kick in the hole at an early age for acting like a gobshite. In most cases, it is the mothers of gobshites who coddle them, protect them from criticism and indulge them in the notion that 'everyone is being hard on you.' They tell the gobshite to ignore the criticism that they caused the break-in by not locking the back door when they left, rather than demanding they take it on board. It is often the mother who shields the gobshite from a world that will frown on them getting so drunk they vomit on a wedding cake. This kind of parenting is to blame for roughly 80 per cent of the gobshites we see in the world today. In this chapter, we will examine some of the mistakes that mothers make when raising gobshites.

MOTHERS WHO RAISE GOBSHITES TEND TO...

Ignore Disciplinary Notes Home from School

'Those teachers are awful hard on him.' 'How was he to know not to walk across the wet cement?' 'Sure aren't kids that age meant to be having fun? I think they just want robots in that school.' Sentences like this go into the hard drive of a gobshite and form the basis of the confidence that runs their operating system. These are the same sentences they will spout later in life when appearing before disciplinary boards. Ask any primary school teacher about the gobshites in their classroom. The common thread among them all, aside from attempting to eat glue, is parents who think they can do no wrong. (Each year the education system loses thousands of teachers to gobshite-related incidents. It's death by a thousand gobshite cuts. Educators across the globe can only take so much from the gobshites they are attempting to teach. Every teacher has a tipping point.) Meeting the parents of a gobshite who has been making your classroom a misery is a challenge that no teaching college mentions to its students. If they did, the already chronically low numbers of good people entering the teaching profession would be far lower again. When a teacher sends a note home to a parent about their child refusing to pee into the toilet, attempting to strap the class turtle to a toy car or kicking a child in the vagina, the response is either stereo silence or complete disbelief. The overwhelming sense of 'what's the fucking point?' that this gives teachers is often too much to bear.

Over-Compliment Their Child

'He really is a very special boy. He put his socks in the laundry basket.' Gobshites often believe they deserve more credit for doing basic shit the rest of us take as normal, standard practice or the bare minimum. This belief stems from mothers who set the bar for praiseworthy behaviour so low that these gobshites spend the rest of their lives thinking they deserve a medal for paying their rent. The impact of over-complimenting a young gobshite is deep and resonates through their bizarre and unfounded sense of self-confidence for the rest of their life. 'Why is everyone so mad at me over the car being broken into? I think I should get some credit for not letting the car get stolen.' Only a gobshite who has been over-praised as a child would think that not being completely negligent is a badge of honour.

Defend Their Gobshite Child at All Costs

Mothers of gobshites think that the world is out to get their child, and that it is their role to act as their attorney in all instances. Their gobshite son smashes a precious ornament in a relation's house when moments earlier he was warned not to play with it: 'Ah would ya stop, it was only an old trinket. Would you leave him alone. He's only a child.' Their gobshite daughter nearly poisons the family with her under-cooked chicken: 'You lot need to toughen up. I loved the dinner. Now if you'll excuse me I need to visit the ladies' room for a few hours.' As long as a gobshite child has a powerful voice saying, 'They're not that bad' or 'How was he to know the cat was that flammable?', their behaviour will become ingrained. Their worldview becomes skewed towards the thinking that when things go wrong, it is not their fault. They are never the sole cause of something breaking, smashing, falling apart or becoming a legal matter.

Brag About Their Gobshite Child

Humility is not a word associated with the mothers of gobshites. Their view of their child is so disconnected from reality that they will spend much of each day telling friends, family and anyone who will listen that 'he's actually doing great on the parole system. They said he's the best lad they've ever had connected to a crime like this.' The contradictions embedded in the praise are invisible to a gobshite's mother. 'He told me that he finished top of the class or at least his section of the class.' They don't hear what we hear. That is down to one very simple thing.

Believe Everything Their Gobshite Child Tells Them

A gobshite can tell their mother they invented the iPhone and they would believe them. If someone took issue with this, the mother would say, 'Well, he might as well have invented it. He is an absolute wizard when it comes to the technology.' The extent to which a gobshite's mother trusts every word that comes out of their mouth is as astonishing as it is infuriating for the siblings of the gobshite. 'He told me there were no more flowers left in the shop. He tried to get me flowers for Mother's Day and that's all that matters.' Warning: Mothers of gobshites become enraged at the suggestion that their gobshite child could be lying to them. Insinuating that a gobshite might have told their mother a half-truth or was economical with the truth is one way to send them into a blind rage. 'Why do you have such a dim view of your brother? I know he wouldn't lie to me about something like this. He was served a bad pint last night. And that is the end of it.'

Believe the Siblings of Their Gobshite Child Are Jealous of Him

Why would the brothers and sisters of someone who can't hold down a job or a relationship be jealous of that person? It makes no sense to anyone other than the mother of that gobshite. A mother might say to the brother who won multiple track and field medals and was immensely popular locally, 'You've always had green eyes when it comes to your sister. If it wasn't her medals for athletics, it was the way all the neighbours liked her and not you. You could never be happy for her.' This twisting of the truth and reclaiming of the siblings' achievements in the name of the gobshite is very common. Don't get drawn in. It will only lead to further accusations of jealousy or worse.

Have Very Foggy Memories

'Ah, I remember, your brother brought me tea in bed before school each day. He was such a little topper.' A gobshite's mother might say this when it was the sibling who brought the tea in bed and the gobshite was the one who had to be dragged kicking and screaming from the scratcher each day. Gobshite parents need to recalibrate reality in order to convince themselves they didn't completely fuck up in raising such an unemployable problem child.

Golden Child Gobshite

Why do gobshites get food poisoning more than any group in the world today? Why do more gobshites fall out of trees and sustain life changing head injuries? Why do so many gobshites leap to their deaths on their first day attempting parkour? The answer is not 'because they're gobshites'. The answer lies in their troubling level of self-confidence. Only a gobshite would be unfazed by electrocuting themselves multiple times a week. Only a gobshite can walk away, swagger undiminished, from a relationship that ended with their partner saying talking to them was a kind of torture. Why do gobshites believe in themselves so much? The rest of us walk around doubting our instincts, second guessing our gut feeling, expertise, knowledge and judgement on things we are more than capable of doing. Why are there so many gobshites on this planet convinced that the world needs to hear their input when, time and time again, their contribution has been identified, often in court, as the main reason everything around them went up in flames?

Only a person who was raised as the golden child of the family can grow up to be an adult gobshite with an unshakable belief in themselves as 'an absolute legend', genius, hilarious human, life and soul of the party and all-round hero, despite all the evidence to the contrary. It's pretty simple and it happens very early on in life. When a child receives praise for doing fuck all, it warps their view of both themselves and the world's expectations of them.

If you tell a young boy he's a 'great lad' for putting his plate in the dishwasher, there's no harm in that, right? What if everyone else contributed to making the dinner and he did absolutely nothing to help other than lie on the couch watching football? What if, under these circumstances, his parents tell him he's 'the most thoughtful, hard-working and considerate fella in this house' for putting his plate in the dishwasher? What is the result of doing that day in, day out for years? Well, for starters his siblings will loathe him and feel a lingering sense of injustice for their entire lives. The outcome for the young boy is a self-satisfied belief that even though his contribution might be small, it's of greater value than that of everyone else. No comment is passed when his sibling fills the fridge with groceries. He arrives in with one carton of milk and his parents throw an impromptu tea party where everyone must comment on how fabulous and fresh the milk tastes. His sister graduates from medical school and neither parent can quite remember the event. He wins a hamper in a local raffle and his decision to buy two tickets rather than one is hailed for years to come as the mark of his high IQ.

The gobshite confidence of a golden child is stronger than oak and as shallow as the paddling pool in which he apparently proved he could swim. Through over-praising, parents of a golden child create a monster gobshite who will never fully comprehend why others cannot see their genius, kindness, attractiveness and humour the way their mother and father do. But the deepest disservice this type of parenting does for the child in question takes place when they cover for the golden child's horrendous mistakes, errors, catastrophic events and fuck-ups.

He might lose his job in a warehouse for gross negligence and never fully understand his culpability simply because the narrative his parents gave him was, 'That manager always had it in for him. They knew he'd be running the place in the space of two years. I think they set him up.' He might have a terrible breakup with a girlfriend when she finds out he has an active profile on a dating app. He will never understand how wrong this is because his parents will say, 'That girl was so controlling. I think it's desperate. She wouldn't let him have a Facebook profile.' Another girl might break up with him due to his poor hygiene but it will enter the family lore as another time when a woman 'could not accept him for the gorgeous boy that he is.'

From childhood onwards, the golden boy gobshite fails to see himself as the cause of any of his problems. Every 'how was I supposed to know?' moment can be traced back to their formative years. Every road collision they are responsible for. Every time a bouncer throws them out of a nightclub. Every time they drink while on medication despite having been warned by their doctor not to. Every time a dog they antagonise eventually bites them. Every time they deem it a good idea to tell an airport security guard that he seems to be in a bad mood. Every penalty for that tax return they claimed contained 'most of their details'. Every surprise party they ruin, gift they mistakenly unwrap, Mother's Day they forget, woman who isn't pregnant they insult, historical monument they desecrate and storm of annoyance in which they are the centre – it all emanates from the golden child pedestal from which they were conditioned to view the world.

DEALING WITH A
GOLDEN CHILD GOBSHITE

In the family setting, unfortunately, there is very little you can do other than find a towel to bite into in the bathroom and a good chunky pillow to yell into in your bedroom. Those two approaches have helped generations of siblings of gobshites cope with the stress and anger of a gobshite brother or sister who thinks their shit don't stink.

Your challenge is to resist the temptation of trying to convince your parents that the golden child is a gobshite. Asking yourself, 'When will they see what a gobshite this person is?' is as much of a waste of time and energy as asking a golden child gobshite to help with the clean-up after Christmas dinner. You can do it if you like but it's never going to happen. Your parents have their view of you and their view of the gobshite. It's hard enough to get parents to change the channel on the television, never mind their perception of their own offspring. There is no magic wand that will make them appreciate your thoughtful gestures, rather than compare them negatively to the pathetic excuses for gestures conducted by your gobshite sibling. If the golden child gobshite gives your parents a refuse bag full of pens stolen from his office for Christmas and you give them a crystal vase just like the one your gobshite sibling broke all those years ago, you will be demonised for bringing up the past and the gobshite will be lauded for being so clever and saving so much money.

Parental Reactions to Gifts from
Gobshite Golden Child *vs* a Regular child

GIFTS FROM GOLDEN CHILD	GIFTS FROM NORMAL CHILD
Set of car seat covers	*Hand-crafted family tree artwork*

↓ ↓

'How did you know I'd like this? You're a little topper.'

'Why in the name of God did you waste so much time on this?'

↓ ↓

PLACEMENT	PLACEMENT
Immediately placed in car, photos taken, toast raised at dinner in the good sitting room	*Stuffed behind a cupboard*

15

Global
Gobshite Events

Certain events attract gobshites. Some events even require
gobshites to participate in them. Some events were created
by gobshites for other gobshites. Regular people, with
common sense, often attend such events to a marvel at
the gobshites involved. The spectacle of hundreds or even
thousands of gobshites engaging in gobshite behaviour in an
organised (if chaotic) setting is mesmerising.

THE RUNNING OF THE BULLS, SPAIN

Do you like cruelty to animals? Do you like seeing gobshites
getting gored by animals they have been cruel to? If so,
you're going to love the Running of the Bulls in Pamplona.
The ancient tradition is as old as it is stupid. Some gobshite
releases a load of bulls into the streets. Gobshites from all
over the world who view themselves as 'brave' torment
the animals and attempt to run in front of them as they are
herded to the bullring outside the city. The one positive of
the entire event is the carnage – dozens of gobshites getting
the kick in the hole they so desperately deserve. The fact
that these men and women return year on year to take part
despite the horrific injuries is proof, if proof was needed, that
gobshites never learn.

CHEESE ROLLING IN GLOUCESTERSHIRE, UK

At the top of a ridiculously steep hill somewhere in the English countryside some gobshite releases a round cheese that then rolls down the incline while hordes of other gobshites race to catch it. These gobshites lose their footing almost immediately, roll, flip, bounce and buckle themselves attempting to be the first to 'catch the cheese'. Many gobshites have dislocated and broken limbs but that, as the gobshites who organise this event say, 'is all part of the fun'.

LA TOMATINA, SPAIN

On the final Wednesday in August, every year, regardless of how many people are living in poverty, thousands of Spanish gobshites descend upon Buñol, Spain, to engage in the world's dumbest food festival. One hundred tons of overly ripe tomatoes are distributed around the city for gobshites to throw at each other in the world's biggest food fight event. Naturally, all the gobshites leave town before the clean-up has even begun.

THE CASTELLS DE TARRAGONA (THE HUMAN TOWER COMPETITION), SPAIN

Remember when you made a five-man human pyramid for a photo when you were fifteen? Everyone told you to stop but it was a bit of fun until your friend Thomas burst himself off the top of it and your wrist took ages to come right afterwards? Well, in Tarragona, Spain, each and every year, gobshites who never learned the lesson it took you 15 minutes to learn as a child gather to hurt themselves building human towers. They will tell you it is the 'ultimate test of strength, balance and courage' but anyone with eyes can see it is an acid test for gobshite DNA.

EL COLACHO (THE BABY JUMPING FESTIVAL), SPAIN

If there's one thing Spain loves it's to gather gobshites together for pointless events that put the lives of others at risk. In El Colacho, fully fledged grown-up gobshites dress up as the devil and then attempt to run and jump over babies belonging to other gobshites. Thousands of spectators flock to the town each year thinking the same thing as you: 'This can't be real.' Sadly it is. Gobshites believe that if a baby does not get jumped over it will live its life constantly looking over its shoulder.

THE ATHERSTONE BALL GAME, ENGLAND

Each year the greatest gobshites in the United Kingdom gather in the town of Atherstone to knock seven shades of shite out of each other. They claim it's a ball game of some sort but really it's just a mass brawl where a reinforced beach ball is the focus. The streets of this quaint English town heave with the hordes of gobshites who jostle, punch, drag, kick and wrestle each other to get close to the ball. What then? Once someone has the ball the crowd descends upon this person and batters them until they release it. If there was a test to see if an English person is a gobshite, taking part in this brain-dead event would be it.

16

How Is That Gobshite on the Television?

There is a rich and profitable history of portraying gobshites on screen. These depictions help us to understand the gobshites in our lives and perhaps feel less bad about their prominence. If Chandler can put up with Joey, maybe you can put with Sean in accounts. Then again, Joey Tribbiani never ruined your chances of a promotion by saying you dared him to photocopy his penis at the Christmas party. That was all Sean's idea, but incredibly, nobody believes he was capable of that original thought.

MICHAEL SCOTT (*THE OFFICE*)

The American version of *The Office* is built on the premise that the boss is a complete and utter gobshite. Steve Carell's performance as Michael so perfectly encapsulated the American corporate gobshite that the show became a comfort blanket for all those who have had to deal with corporate incompetence. Michael Scott captures that quintessential gobshite trait of self-belief. Michael believes he is hilarious despite the multiple formal warnings he has received from David Wallace for inappropriate humour. Michael believes himself to be a shrewd investor despite his bankruptcy and spending on what Oscar calls 'things nobody needs'. He believes himself to be a great judge of character despite the fact that the guy he hired as a temp would eventually be arrested for embezzlement. Like all the truly great gobshites, Michael Scott has a resilience that is hard to believe. No matter how embarrassing the event or scheme, he somehow appears on the other side with a gormless smile. And somehow, in spite of all of this, like a lot of gobshites, he is infuriatingly likable.

FATHER DOUGAL MAGUIRE (*FATHER TED*)

Few characters in the history of stage and screen have captured the essence of a gobshite better than Father Dougal Maguire. Dougal is the kind of high-end gobshite who could not be trusted with a butter knife. Many observers expressed disbelief or even anger at the depiction of the Irish via Maguire. The truth, and the reason the character resonated in the way he did, was that everyone in Ireland knew 'a Dougal'. Those who wrote the character clearly understood certain gobshites. Dougal's talent lay in his ability to say the wrong thing at the absolute wrong time. At the time of airing, Fr Dougal set the gobshite bar for idiotic behaviour in Ireland and the UK. During the mid-nineties, his name entered the vernacular as a standard of stupidity. If a person was clueless or lost or said something incongruous they were said to be 'doing a Father Dougal' or 'being a bit of Father Dougal today'. Its impression was so powerful that, according to Ardal O'Hanlon, the actor who played him, to this day, people assume he is a gobshite in real life.

HOMER SIMPSON (*THE SIMPSONS*)

The head of the Simpson household might be the greatest animated gobshite of all time. His level of ignorance and stupidity are only matched by his ability to wind up in situations where he has been entrusted with too much responsibility. Homer is that gobshite we all know who keeps getting hired. Every time you meet them they have some new thing they're about to do. You look forward to meeting them again so that you can hear how it went up in flames. It is a mystery as to how Homer is still alive. His level of gobshitery has entered the level of fine art in that he is like a painter weaving chaotic capers with every breath he takes. Like all of the most extraordinary gobshites in the world, it is almost mesmerising to watch Homer move through the world.

FRANK SPENCER
(*SOME MOTHERS DO 'AVE 'EM*)

Frank is the agent of chaos gobshite who is trying his absolute best to make a life for his family while simultaneously setting fire to the world around him. He leaves a trail of destruction in his wake and drives all those who interact with him to distraction. When he first appeared on British TV screens, he was an instant sensation. The BBC had created less of a comedy show and more of a wildlife documentary about a gobshite. Michael Crawford's stellar performance as Frank won him numerous awards and accolades. Today Frank Spencer is still a standard reference for 'gobshite' throughout the UK. 'Whoopsies', as he called them, referred to any kind of gobshite-related unfortunate event.

HYACINTH BUCKET
(*KEEPING UP APPEARANCES*)

Hyacinth is the type of gobshite who is trying to fool the world into thinking she is something she clearly is not. In the BBC comedy series, she is the quintessential British snob dead set on showing the neighbours exactly how well she's doing in spite of all the evidence to the contrary. Pronouncing her name 'Bouquet' is just the tip of her gobshite iceberg. Her character resonated with every viewer who had ever encountered a gobshite on a crusade to look better than those around them. Like all these gobshites, Hyacinth is blissfully unaware of how she is coming off. She lives in a bungalow. She does not have staff yet she answers the phone, 'The Bouquet residence; the lady of the house speaking.' Hyacinth may be the most accurate female gobshite character ever created.

Gobshites Behind the Wheel

It is hard to believe that there is no gobshite test associated with learning to drive. Especially when we consider the number of gobshite-related collisions, 'accidents' and road rage incidents they cause. Insurance companies have known for years that gobshites struggle to drive cars safely and yet they have a very high success rate in passing the test to obtain a driving licence. You would be forgiven for thinking that insurance providers would think twice about insuring individuals who struggle to fasten their safety belt, let alone keep their car on the right side of the road. On the contrary, these companies have actively encouraged gobshites to drive so they can raise premiums and punish those who are not distracted by squirrels while behind the wheel.

But how do we spot a gobshite driving a car? There are so many telltale signs. Here is a list police across the world have been using for decades: ten dead giveaway signs that the person you're dealing with is a gobshite operating a road vehicle.

I. NO LICENCE

Many gobshites drive without a licence. If you ask them about their licence, they will put their finger over their lips or wink at you.

2. EXPIRED LICENCE

Renewing things is not something gobshites tend to do. Many do not even know that a licence needs to be renewed. They will say, 'I have a licence though.' Or, 'Ah, come on, how was I supposed to know?' Expiry dates cause gobshites major issues. Failure to read expiry dates is the number one reason why gobshites wind up in hospital so much. It's the same reason why gobshites make terrible chefs.

3. DRIVING AT HIGH SPEED

If you gave a gobshite a radio, the first thing they would do is turn it up full blast. If you gave a gobshite an elastic band, they would attempt to stretch it to its fullest extent. They take the same approach with road vehicles. A car, just like the elastic band, is too much responsibility to give a gobshite. Knowing when to stop is one of life's biggest struggles for gobshites.

4. LIGHTS UNDERNEATH THE VEHICLE

If a car's underside is glowing, chances are there's a gobshite driving it. It's quite astonishing the effort gobshites go to when it comes to enhancing their car's appearance when in all other areas of their life they are a complete fucking shambles.

5. EXTRA LOUD EXHAUST PIPE

A loud exhaust is like a glowing yellow arrow above the car letting you know there is a gobshite inside. For years, car manufacturers had assumed all drivers wanted their cars to be quieter. They spent billions on technology to reduce the sound emitted by the engine and exhaust system. High-powered racing cars were the exception; it made no sense to waste time or energy on that stuff for them because the race track is so fucking loud anyway. But gobshites saw these cars and thought, 'That's cool.' It's that simple. They think it's cool to have a car that sounds like it needs a service. Forget the noise pollution of it. Forget the fact that everywhere they go people look at them and their car with genuine anger. Gobshites are unencumbered by any thoughts for other people a lot of the time. This is just another one of those times.

6. PARKING

You and I try our very best to get our car to fit between the two white lines of a parking space. Not gobshites. There is a kind of gobshite illiteracy when it comes to parking spaces where they simply can't quite make out what is expected of them. Parking two inches from the neighbouring car, across three spaces or with the arse of the car jutting out into the road are just three of the gobshite parking traditions. It is estimated that 70 per cent of the world's parking tickets are given to gobshites. When asked, most gobshites believe themselves to be great at parking in spite of the scrapes and dints all over their cars.

7. SCRAPES ON THE VEHICLE

A gobshite's bumper or fender is always covered in scrapes, paint from other cars and dints. They believe that this is what a bumper is for. They think that the bumper is used to identify when you can go no further or when to stop accelerating. Gobshites use the bumper on their car as a type of low-grade antenna to establish when they are about to hit something. If there's a scrape on your car, chances are a gobshite didn't just do it, they thought it was a good idea.

8. LACK OF CONCENTRATION

Holding a gobshite's attention is very tricky, even when they are operating a deadly machine. Gobshites have a lot going on in their heads. They struggle to deal with one thing at a time –

driving is many things all at once. For a gobshite that's a fucking nightmare. Most gobshite-related accidents in the workplace and behind the wheel are a result of a gobshite thinking of or seeing something. They see a billboard, they forget to stop at the lights. They are at the lights, they are listening to the radio, they forget to go when the lights turn green.

9. INDICATORS ARE OPTIONAL

Gobshites think telling other road users what they are about to do is like holding the door for an old lady. You don't have to do it but it's nice to do it sometimes. This drives the rest of us fucking crazy.

10. BLAMING EVERYONE ELSE

If a gobshite is in a collision it can take an entire court case to convince them they were at fault. If you are crashed into or blindsided by a gobshite going too fast or not looking where he was going, the first thing you will hear are the words, 'What were you doing?'

Sometimes we encourage the right to free speech because it helps us identify the gobshites among us. We let gobshites talk so that they can reveal themselves to us. Car parks fulfill a similar purpose. Spotting the gobshites in a crowd might be hard but in car park it's easy. The car park is a canvas all gobshites enjoy exploring. Below we can see three gobshites. Two are obvious and one is less clear. The badly parked gobshite is the most obvious. The task of parking is so simple. Insert your vehicle between the two lines. The first difficulty for the gobshite is that parking requires thought for others. This as we have learned, is not their strong suit. The motorcyclist has parked across a space for differently abled drivers because he or she believes that this space is given on first come first served basis. They may later contend to a parking warden that they are in fact differently abled because they have psoriasis. The third gobshite appears to have parked perfectly well. Can you tell what makes them a gobshite? Look closely. This gobshite has borrowed friend's car. They have left their lights on. The battery will be dead when they return. They will call their friend to explain what happened and swear that they did turn the lights off and that 'there must be something wrong with the car.'

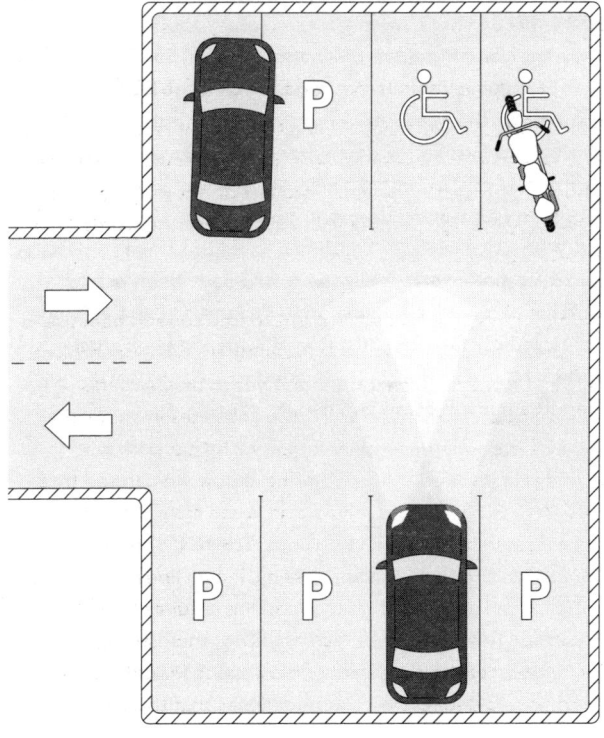

GOBSHITES AT THE HELM

A gobshite in a car is one thing, but what happens when one is in charge of a large passenger vessel?

There are gobshites who say a lot of things and there are gobshites who believe a lot of things. Captain Edward Smith believed his ship, the *Titanic*, was indestructible because it was big. Of all the gobshite things to think about a ship sailing at full speed through an ice field, this was on a new level of dumb and cost the lives of 1,517 people including Leonardo DiCaprio's great-grandfather and Kate Winslet's great-granny. In the 1997 James Cameron documentary about the tragedy, when the call of 'iceberg dead ahead' came, Smith wasn't even at his post. Rumour has it he ordered the engine room to speed up the boat. Like a boxer violently jerking his head forward and into an oncoming punch, Smith will forever be regarded as one of history's biggest gobshites as a result of his hubris, and for ruining the potential marriage of the DiCaprio and Winslet families. All Smith had to do was point the *Titanic* towards America and everyone would have been happy. We'd probably still be sailing on her to this day and enjoying the incredibly talented offspring of Kate and Leo's great-grandparents. But no, Smith decided to sail the boat through a mountain made of ice and he was wrong.

18

Famous Irish People Who Are Not Gobshites in Spite of What People Say

BONO

Anyone who labels Bono a gobshite is a gobshite in my opinion. Bono put a band together with his friends from school, made music that became beloved by the world and earned hundreds of millions of dollars in the process. Most people would retire to an island in the Caribbean and say good luck to everyone. According to these dopes, what makes Bono a gobshite is that he chose to speak out on issues of injustice, intolerance and poverty. He chose to use his platform to raise millions for those worst off in the world. I know. What a bastard. Bono is human. Occasionally he makes mistakes. He does and says silly things sometimes. He wears regrettable outfits and has had quite a few dodgy haircuts. Does that make him a gobshite? The short answer is no.

MATTRESS MICK

Mick is a man who sells beds and mattresses in huge quantities to Irish people. He has done this for years and built a business empire. To promote his work he has created some goofy ads in the same vein as a typical used car salesman might in America. This has led many Irish people to label him a gobshite. But nothing could be further from the truth. Mattress Mick has a self-awareness and ability to poke fun at himself no gobshite has ever possessed. His business prowess is undeniable. He might even be the opposite of a gobshite. Irish people have a term for a person who is the other end of the gobshite spectrum: they call them 'a cute hoor'. Mick is cute for sure. He is well aware that some people laugh at him and his over-the-top billboards and persona – but Mick knows it's good for business so he doubles down on it. A gobshite could never do that.

THE HEALY-RAES

The genius of the Healy-Raes is they have the world convinced they are gobshites when they are anything but. The Healy-Rae family has been in Irish politics for generations. For decades these men have been solving the problems of their constituents faster than you can say, 'Where are they holding the afters for the funeral?' Write them off at your peril.

19

Arguing with a Gobshite

A direct route to madness, playing handball against a haystack, the definition of stupidity – call it what you like; arguing with a gobshite is an infuriating experience with no winners. The saddest part is that gobshites demand you argue with them. 'Why are we not allowed to use the same cloth to clean the cups as I used to wipe the floor?' 'I know the camera says I was the last one to leave but I wasn't.' 'Why is it my job to feed the dog when you're not here?' Questions about things nobody else needs clarity on, pushing back on things that were previously agreed, quizzing you on things that nobody else has a problem with – a gobshite will seek out a pointless argument like a shark smelling blood in the water. They think it's all part of the day. Gobshites view arguments the way the rest of us view washing our hands. Incidentally, gobshites rarely wash their hands. In this chapter we will examine the principal difficulties faced when trying to argue with a gobshite. Is it worth our while at all?

THE SUBJECT OF THE ARGUMENT MAY NOT MAKE ANY SENSE

'Why are you getting so mad at me? I know I'm the only one with the keys but why is this my job?' The thing to bear in

The Gobshite's Self-Image Compared to the Level of Annoyance They Cause

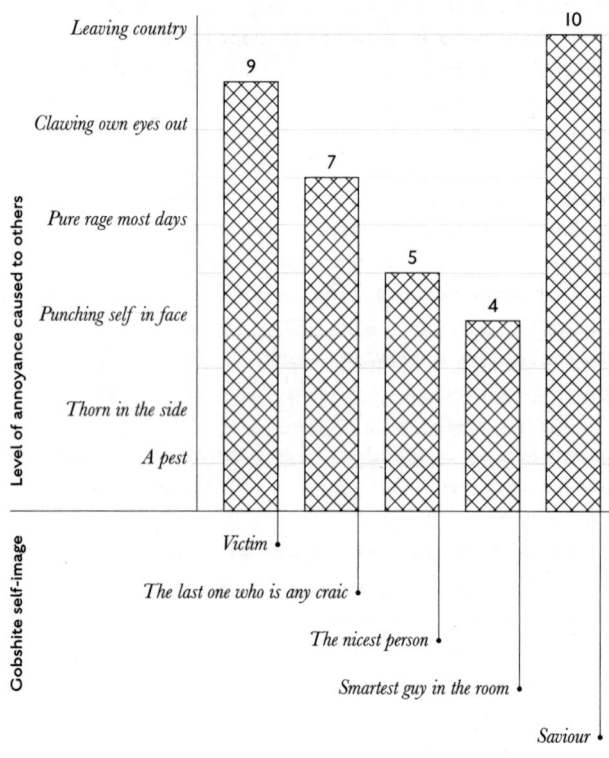

mind when arguing with a gobshite is that what appears obvious is not obvious to them. For this reason, 'Why can't you see?' is the dumbest thing you can say in an argument with a gobshite. They can't see because they are a gobshite and nothing is plain and simple for them. A lot of your time arguing with a gobshite will be devoted to getting clear on the basic or bare minimum. Dogs need food. Carbon monoxide is poisonous. You're not supposed to look into the barrel of a gun. Flies are not okay around food. That smell is not good. Your mother could not have done this for you in the past. The internet is not in the computer. Dirt doesn't improve your immune system. If you venture down the path of arguing with a gobshite, get ready to explain some basic shit for a long time.

EVEN WHEN YOU WIN, YOU LOSE

You might walk away from an argument with a gobshite and think to yourself, 'Well, at least I got through to him in the end.' You didn't. He may say, 'Fine, I get it, alright, I'm sorry' but he is not fine. Neither does he get it. He certainly isn't sorry. The gobshite is in a lot of cases simply trying to end the argument. Think back on the arguments you've had with gobshites. Did you win or did they just pull the escape cord? It's a demoralising fact that when gobshites are in arguments they forget what the argument was about the moment it ends. So if your gobshite teenage son got in a big argument with you over leaving his hairdryer plugged in and the risk that posed of burning down the house, he might do it again tomorrow. Why? Because by the time you explained to him what was wrong with what he did, he will have forgotten why these comments were being directed at him. He was thinking about other things that could set the house on fire and why they don't need to be unplugged. The days of a gobshite are made up of moving from one calamity to the next, so they have a tremendous capacity to rearview mirror a lot of things. A gobshite could crash a school bus, be arrested for dangerous driving, get bailed out and still really enjoy their dinner that evening.

THE GOBSHITE VIEWS HIMSELF AS THE VICTIM

Even if they burned the school down, even if they poisoned everyone at work with the cake they found on the side of the street, even if they and they alone deleted the hard drive, a gobshite will see the entire experience through the prism of them being the person who has fared out the worst from it. 'How do you think I feel in all of this, lads?' 'Nobody told me not to pull the trigger. I should have been told it was a real gun.' 'How was I to know?' The gobshite thinks that pulling them up on their terrible behaviour is a form of abuse and that arguing with them over it is even worse. Once you attempt to bring a gobshite into line, you need to expect them to tell you that you're being aggressive and over the top. 'There's no sign saying grown-ups shouldn't go down the slide. I don't know why you're being like this with me when all I was trying to do was have a bit of fun.' Crying and looking sad are the high end of this behaviour. Telling a gobshite to stop crying can further inflame the victim mentality and makes engaging in the argument impossible.

THE RESPONSES YOU GET WILL MAKE YOU MORE AND MORE ANGRY

The responses of a gobshite, when you are attempting to present them with an alternative point of view, will drive you over the edge. Even if you started the argument with your gobshite on an even keel. Even if you are taking your blood pressure medication and practising transcendental meditation three times a day. Be ready.

They failed to secure insurance for the event they organised and are now being investigated: 'The whole thing is rigged anyway.' The Food Safety Authority told them that maggots were found in their kitchen: 'I don't know, I think everyone is too uptight these days.' They stood you up on a date: 'Why didn't you just go to the cinema on your own? Do I have to hold your hand while you do everything?'

20

Spotting Gobshites Online

The internet is the breeding ground, principal refuge and playpen of the gobshite. Its veil of anonymity allows gobshites to trick regular people into treating them with a respect they do not deserve. The fact that entry to the internet is free gives all gobshites the opportunity to comment upon events, professions and subjects they know sweet fuck all about. Most of all, the internet provides gobshites with a unique sanctuary in which they can meet, befriend and feel emboldened by other gobshites. The jury is still out on whether the internet changed the world for the better; when viewed through the prism of the rise of the gobshite in the world, it has been a complete and utter disaster.

BEFORE THE WORLD WIDE WEB GOBSHITES WERE QUIET PEOPLE

As hard as it is to believe, there was a time before smartphones, 24-hour on-demand porn, streaming platforms, social media and a comments section under every news story. When news appeared on the TV, radio and newspaper, gobshites kept a lot of their opinions to themselves. They had the same bullshit thoughts as today but they had very few places to go with them. 'They should just shoot all the people that are in jail.' 'I don't think there should be speed limits.' 'There is a good chance there are aliens here already.' 'My mate Dave is stronger than the Incredible Hulk.' 'A lot of these comic book characters are based on true stories but the government doesn't want us to know about this stuff.'

Gobshites could think what they liked and the only time you had to listen to them was if you were unfortunate enough to wind up on a bus with them, sitting next to them at a wedding, or listening to a late-night radio phone-in show. You might not be aware of this but about 30 years ago when radio stations were struggling to get people to listen late at night, they invited gobshites on the air to vent their views on the subjects of the day or anything that caught their fancy. It was riveting stuff. In terms of fun ways to pass the time, it was also a great alternative to hammering nails through your genitals.

LATE-NIGHT PHONE-IN RADIO SHOWS

Before the internet, gobshites had two places to let it all out: the pub and these radio shows. Just as in the pub, where the bar owner profited off the gobshite's inability to shut the fuck up while making approximately zero sense, the radio station owners did the same. The model was as simple as selling gobshites alcohol. Give a gobshite a rope and he thinks he's a cowboy. Give a gobshite some air time and he thinks the world wants to listen. Was it exploitative to have gobshites spouting nonsense on the airwaves to each other, each and every night? Were gobshites qualified to speak at length on subjects such as teen promiscuity, crime, dogs, the rise in the cost of running a taxi, foreigners, foreigners driving taxis and the injustices gobshites felt they had suffered? It didn't matter. Gobshites could be sequestered and put in the late-night chat show echo chamber and safely away from the rest of us. It was good to let them get it all out of their system. It made them feel like their unfounded, contradictory and often racist opinions mattered. And we all got to listen, laugh and wonder, 'Where are they finding these gobshites?'

The truth was, locating these gobshites was not that difficult. The DJs and research teams hired on these shows were experts in luring gobshites onto the air, finding topics that piqued the gobshite community's interest and drawing them out on subjects they knew nothing about but loved nonetheless. Swans attacking children, teens dressing inappropriately, foreigners attacking swans, the list goes on. Once late-night radio was established as a congregation point for gobshites, the community flowed towards it like sheep to fresh grass. (Side note: Sheep are regarded by other animals as the biggest gobshites of the animal kingdom.)

SO WHEN DID GOBSHITES EMBRACE THE INTERNET?

For decades, radio was the preferred platform of the gobshite, for the very same reasons the internet would become their favoured stomping ground for pedalling their half-baked bullshit ideas:

1) Any gobshite could get access.

2) All the gobshites on the air were anonymous.

3) Being broadcast gave the gobshite credibility.

4) It was hard for those in charge to shut the gobshite up.

5) There was no pesky fact checking – if challenged a gobshite would just say, 'I'm entitled to my own opinion' or, 'I didn't interrupt you. Let me finish.'

The same five facts drew them online. The gobshite wants to be heard because they have spent much of their life watching people's eyes glaze over while they are talking. They want to remain anonymous so they can share whatever shite comes into their head without having to face any consequences, such as how that shite might make others feel. They want credibility because most people in their lives have dismissed them as a gobshite within a few minutes of hearing them speak. They want free rein to blather on without anyone interrupting them. Again, this is a constant in their life and they want to be free of it. And finally, gobshites don't want to hear evidence, research or objective truths. Those things tend to make it difficult for them to take wild swings on subjects they know nothing about and are often the reason they lost their court case or most recent job.

The internet provided all of those things in spades. The first place they found it online was in what were called 'chat rooms'. A complete misnomer if ever there was one. From their inception, online chat rooms were crawling with gobshites with absolutely no filter, manners, knowledge or sense that 'maybe people don't need to hear this'. Then social media platforms took the chat room and said, 'How can we make this more attractive to gobshites?'

GOBSHITES ON SOCIAL MEDIA: IN THE BEGINNING

In the beginning, social media was a bit of a joke. 'Why would anyone want to hear what I have to say?' was the prevailing opinion among people who had never dreamed of taking a picture of their breakfast. Twitter, as it was then known, was likened to a group of people shouting out the windows of their houses random shit that passersby didn't need to hear. 'Just had the best walk with my dog. Ohh Saturdays are the best.' 'What's the deal with kettles these days taking so long to boil?' It was believed in 2005 that Facebook, Bebo, MySpace and the like were just a flash in the pan. Once people got over the fact that they could now broadcast their most inane thoughts, they'd get back to work and, more important, back to using their smartphones for what they were intended – looking up the opening hours of bakeries, restaurants and stores you intended to visit and getting directions to these establishments.

We had a glorious future to look forward to of not getting lost and not standing out in the rain asking the question, 'Who the fuck doesn't open on a Monday?' But then something terrible happened. The companies behind the social media websites recognised that 90 per cent of the 'early adopters' of their technology were spending most of their time in the comments or replies section getting in arguments with other users. Just like in real life, in the online world gobshites were soaking up the time of regular people by challenging them ('There's no way you took that photo'), antagonising them ('Typical comment from a woman') and telling them they had no sense of humour after making problematic jokes ('FFS you're so serious, lighten up for God's sake, that tragedy happened years ago. I'm allowed joke about it now').

Rather than booting these gobshites off their new social media spaces, the creators, many of whom were gobshites themselves, actively encouraged gobshites to engage and build a presence on the sites. Mark Zuckerberg and his pals knew that if these gobshites could drag you into a conversation on something they knew nothing about, or about a photo they had posted of you without your permission with the caption 'How does this lad have a girlfriend?', normal folks would stay on longer and invest in these sites.

How to Spot a Gobshite on Social Media

Gobshites are good at hiding in the long grass in a lot of situations. In a relationship, they might wait until the wedding night to truly make a show of themselves at the reception. At work, they might wait until the big deadline to prove they have no fucking clue what they are doing and you take the fall on their behalf. On a bus, they might lure you into a conversation that you can't get out of and then start telling you why they don't like foreigners. If social media has done one positive thing it has allowed us to clearly identify gobshites of all ages quicker than ever before. Here are a few of the most obvious online gobshite giveaways.

'Is this supposed to be funny?'

A comment such as this speaks to the self-importance and complete lack of self-awareness of a gobshite online. The gobshite comment of, 'I think this is shit' can appear under the reviews of the collected works of Charles Dickens. A gobshite believes that the general consensus is irrelevant and that it is their opinion and their opinion only that matters. The gobshite will never stop and say to themselves, 'maybe I'm wrong on this' or 'maybe I'm not seeing what other people are seeing here'. To the gobshite online, all that matters is their first reaction. If a piece of work, writing, music, film or media requires the viewer to invest time to enjoy it, the gobshite will comment 'BOOOOORING. TOO LONG OF AN INTRO.' If the work is fast paced, they'll say, 'I can't understand this, why is it jumping around so much?' If the work is emotional, 'GAAAAAAY' is often the comment.

Spotting gobshites in the comments section is not limited to spotting their nonsensical opinions on things that almost everyone agrees are good.

'I COULD DO THAT'/'I don't get it'

Gobshites have zero respect for the time it takes for anyone to do anything they themselves have not done. You can present a gobshite with a four-course meal and they will say, 'What took so long?' Unless a gobshite does a thing, they can't appreciate that thing. Unless a gobshite is forced to do housework, they will never be able to comprehend that someone actually spends their time cleaning the house, or the effort involved in doing so. This is why courts regularly give gobshites community service rather than prison time. The 'I could do that' comment speaks directly to this. It regularly appears under small posts of something unassuming that might appear on first glance to be 'easy' but which actually involved a lot of expertise and work, like a photo capturing a particular moment. It's equally likely to be found under a graduation photo, marathon story or cancer survivor image. Most gobshites think 'nuance' is a fragrance by Paco Rabanne. The disproportionate and completely baseless nature of a gobshite's self-belief is relentlessly revealed on social media every day of the week. This situation is even worse in the dating app profiles of young gobshite men.

Asking questions they could easily Google

If a gobshite consistently asks you dumb questions in person it's upsetting. When they are holding in their hand a device that gives them access to the answers to all these questions, it's infuriating. 'How much was it?' might appear under a post that contains a detailed price breakdown. 'Is there any way to contact the venue?' you'll find under a post explaining that the venue will be closed for the next few days. 'What time does it start?' under a post detailing the start and end times of the event. 'Can I bring my brother?' under a post about the need to keep attendee numbers low on this occasion.

Whatever it is you are posting about, you can easily spot the gobshites in the comments section by looking for the ones that need confirmation or further explanation of information clearly contained within the post. A gobshite will read the above and comment, 'Yeah, but how do we spot gobshites in terms of the type of questions they ask underneath posts?'

'There's two minutes of my life I'm never getting back'

Snide remarks are what gobshites use as a substitute for humour. Most gobshites have had sarcasm directed at them in the form of the sentence, 'That's a brilliant idea. Why don't you submit it in writing?' After carefully writing down their idea and returning to ask where the suggestion box is, the true nature of the exchange will be explained to the gobshite. From that point on, gobshites will spray their attempts at sarcasm at anyone and everyone regardless of age (kids trying their best), the nature of the relationship (a new acquaintance who doesn't realise they are dealing with a gobshite) or seniority (a manager or boss who could fire them on the spot). 'There's two minutes of my life I'm never getting back' is prime gobshite snark. Nobody ever gets two minutes of their life back. And most gobshites waste the vast majority of their time commenting on videos they could have swiped past two minutes earlier.

Summarising the entire plot in reviews

Gobshites online love to summarise the entire plot of a film or book, including any important plot twist. In fact, they'll often make the plot twist the title of their review to ensure they have ruined the experience for as many people as possible.

ONLINE REVIEWS FROM GOBSHITES

Utter Sh*t Hole Hotel | 6 January 2019 | *The Grand*

I stayed at this hotel and it was absolutely terrible. I stay at a lot of hotels and I have never come across a hotel that was so strict on stupid rules that they had completely made up themselves. I actually think the rules they keept spouting on about to me and the group of gentlemen I was staying with were not even da rules they normally have. We were made feel unwelcome at this hotel even though we had paid the same as everyone else. If you're coming to the city of Galway for a good time avoid this hotel. I sincerely hope your management read this email and that prick on reception.

★ ☆ ☆ ☆ ☆ | Trev69__1966 | Essex

Translation:

This is a pretty typical Tripadvisor review from a gobshite after a stag weekend got out of hand. As gobshites so often do, rather than identifying his group as the problem, they blame the hotel and staff. There are a few tell-tale signs this review is from a complete gobshite, but perhaps the most obvious is when his emotions get the better of him in the final sentence of the review. When he refers to 'the gentlemen I was staying with' he is referring to the gang of yobs who spent the evening in the residents bar singing Oasis songs and screaming 'Oh behave' to any woman who entered the room. When he mentions that he stays at hotels a lot, that is a lie. Here he is limply attempting to say that he is a man of the world who knows how hotels normally work. In truth, he can't remember the last three stag weekends he has been on or the hotels he stayed in because on all three occasions he fell asleep outside and missing his flight home became the focus of his memories.

Not Funny Comedy Club TOTAL JOKE | 18 March 2023 |
Comedy Club Birmingham

Firstly it was not made clear to me that we were not
allowed whisper to each other during the show. THE STAFF
MEMBERS I DEELT WITH WERE SO RUDE THEY WERE
THE ONES MAKING THE MOST NOISE. tHE COMEDIANS
WERE NOT FUNNY WHATSOEVER AND THE FACT THAT
THEY HAD TO KEEP TALKING TO US WAS THE PROVE
OF THAT. we was not drunk. WHEN TEHY ASKED US TO
LEAVE ALL WE DID WAS ASK WHY BUT OHHH NO. an
explanation was not given and they spilled my drink not me.
If you're looking for a comedy club this place is not it. I go
to comedy all the time and I've seen the best comedians on
DVD and out and about.. The common thing they all got is
they can handle people in the crowd who also are funny. Save
yourself a pain in the arsenal and go down your pub with
some mates. Apart fro mthat the show started on time and
the MC guy was really fucking funny. He should have been
on all the time rather than the other four comedians. Also the
music was too loud.

★☆☆☆☆ | MikeHunt1978 | Wales

Translation:
Pretty average review from your standard disruptive
gobshite at a comedy show. There's a clear and obvious
miscommunication here. The gobshite thinks that their
role at the comedy show is to provide the comedian with
fun, spontaneous drunken repartee. He believes that the
comedian's willingness to engage with their moo noises, dull
banter and/or whistling is the measure of how good they
are as a comedian. This is the kind of review that comedians
send each other in WhatsApp groups. The lives of the staff in
comedy clubs are full of interactions with gobshites like these

and we should all spare a thought for them when they are removing gobshites from the building. For us, that is the end of that gobshite. For the staff, the dance has only just begun.

Never Again | 3 July 2024 | *Mackellan Grill & Bistro*

I have been a loyal customer of this place for more than ten years. I'm never going there again and I think nobody should. coZ IT'S SHITE. I got pushed into by a lad behind me in the queue for the counter. I say queue but their system is absolute horse shit. I have seen countless lads getting served ahead of people who have bee n waiting for ages like. And don't get me started on when the guards come in and flash the badge and we're all supposed to just stand to one side.. And I wouldn't mind only they're doing fuck all. There's more crime now than ever before . What the point of a uniformed police man in an unmarked car like. It's so obvious FFS. When I got push into I swung around to see who had pushed and to ask them if they would stop. Whatever way I moved my arms as I turned around I seemed clip one of them lads in the very side of his eye. This threw me off balance and to stop myself from falling over I grabbed the lad (who is a complete prick by the way) by the throat. Next thing is he's kicking me and to try and calm things down I shoved him. If I WANTED SHITE CHIPS ID GO HOME AND MAKE THEM MYSEFL ANYWAY,. tHEY CAN FUCK OFF WITH THEIR CURRY SAUCE AS well my cousin worked there for a week and she said that they steam clean everything every single night and were total dicks about her having to wash her hands all the time. It's a complete mystery to me how they've been in that same shop for a fucking million year.s oh yeah it's not. Its because they've not got a clue what they are doing.

★ ☆ ☆ ☆ ☆ | IrelandForTheIrish88 | Larne

Translation:
When gobshites get in fights in public they usually leave a shitty review of something somewhere to try to claw back some self-respect in their own mind. They then say to people who ask about the fight that someone put up a review of the establishment in which the fight occurred and that the review 'explains a lot'. Many gobshites will have multiple fake accounts on these platforms for this very reason. It doesn't take a detective to figure out what happened in the above scenario.

Once you've started to identify reviews from gobshites it's impossible to stop reading them. Head to TripAdvisor or Amazon and look for the one star reviews of things you know to be fantastic. Reading the reviews of gobshites can can drain the strength of any business person or artist. We can't shut our eyes to their existence. We have to find joy in their despair.

21

Working with Gobshites

THINGS TO KNOW WHEN WORKING WITH A GOBSHITE

At some point in your life, you will find yourself working with one or more gobshites. It's a demoralising realisation, not unlike discovering your house has an unfixable plumbing issue. There's very little you can do about it. You can waste money on getting an expert to examine the problem but there's not a whole lot a plumber or therapist can do for you. You don't get to choose the gobshites you work with. You just have to learn to live with it and try not to punch yourself in the face too many times each day. But is working with gobshites doable? The answer is yes. Working with gobshites can be done if you know these 10 immutable facts. Print this list out or write it down on small cue cards until you have them memorised. These 10 facts will act as a source of calm reassurance for you when you're losing your mind. And they also might provide some answers as to why the gobshites you work with are how they are and, most important, how in the name of Jesus they got hired in the first place.

1) *Nobody wastes time quite like a gobshite.* If there was an Olympic event for time wasting, gobshites would not

just dominate it, they would make the sport a year-round activity. The ability of a gobshite to take more time than necessary to do a simple task is as astonishing as it is upsetting for their colleagues. Give any gobshite a job to do and they will find the longest, least efficient way to do it. And even then you will have to go back and redo the work they have done. You might ask a gobshite to plug in your phone. You might hand the gobshite your phone and a charger. You might think that you have presented them with enough material to complete the task in seconds. You are wrong. A true gobshite will first ask, 'Where do you want me to plug it in?' or, 'Is this the charger you want me to use?' If you think that is the end of this story you have never dealt with a proper gobshite before. The next phase will involve them asking for clarification: 'I can't find an available power socket. Should I unplug something?' Or 'I have it plugged in now but do you want me to turn it on at the wall?' Understand and accept that any job you give a gobshite is going to take twice as long to complete as if you did it yourself. Accept that if you don't assign work to a gobshite, they will not be using their time to do helpful things. This is where the expression 'Will someone give that gobshite something to do' comes from.

2) *Gobshites are bizarrely good in interviews.* You are going to find yourself working with gobshites because for some unknown reason, gobshites interview well. Nobody knows why this is, just as nobody knows why Piers Morgan is on the television. The same rule applies to gobshites on first dates. Their happy-go-lucky attitude can feel attractive on the first viewing. Don't be tricked. A person who seems like they will add to 'the vibe' at your workplace could easily be a gobshite with no intention of ever doing any work whatsoever. Check their references thoroughly. If

any of them are legitimate, you will be warned off hiring them – the only time someone will recommend you hire a gobshite is if they themselves are a gobshite, or if they are trying to offload the problem onto someone else. Too many employers take gobshites and their résumés at face value. Gobshite CVs can read well. Scratch the surface and the shite beneath will be revealed. The gobshite who says he 'left the company to explore new challenges' was told to leave the company because he wasn't up to the challenge of working on reception. The gobshite who says their interests and hobbies are 'going out with friends and the cinema' is trying to tell you they have a drinking problem and spend most of their weekends watching Netflix.

3) *Gobshites will blame you for their fuck-ups.* If you identify a gobshite in your workplace, give them a wide berth. Association with a gobshite is often enough to get you grouped with a gobshite. 'You're friends with that gobshite in accounts, aren't you?' To avoid guilt by association with a gobshite, steer clear. If there's a project or task where you are forced to be in the same working group as a known gobshite, make your excuses and leave work early. Consider taking a sabbatical or sick leave until the project or task is complete. It's the only way to avoid the inevitably disastrous outcome and the blame being laid at your door. Even then, being absent might not be enough to avoid culpability for a gobshite-related dumpster fire at work. Gobshites will point to those who didn't help, those who 'never told me I was meant to calculate the totals for this year and not last year', those who 'made me do all the writing' or those who 'never explained it fully to me'. Avoid befriending or connecting with the gobshites in your workplace at all costs. Never learn their names.

Ignore them when they call you. If they corner you, fake a seizure. There is no other way to avoid them blaming you for their poor performance.

4) **You might be blamed for giving a gobshite work.** 'Who left that gobshite in charge of the forklift?' 'Which one of you fucking eejits let that gobshite submit the form?' 'How many times have I told ye that under no circumstances is that gobshite allowed near the server? He wiped the hard drives. Again!' The mistake of trusting a gobshite in work can get you fired. Right now, as you read this, someone somewhere is in a disciplinary meeting over why they chose the office gobshite for a task this gobshite has proven in the past they could not do. The gobshite does not get the blame for spilling toilet water on the newly installed carpet at reception. The person who asked the gobshite to clean the toilets gets two days' suspension without pay. The hows and whys of the gobshite are not important when working with a gobshite who can barely feed themselves their own lunch. You get the blame for trusting the gobshite.

5) **Gobshites need to be kept busy.** This is harder than it seems. What the hell can you ask a gobshite to do in work that will not result in them setting the building on fire or creating more work that you will have to fix later on? You need to rack your brains for the most straightforward tasks that could go on for hours. Something that gives the gobshite the sense that they are doing something significant. Something that won't break, fall over or result in others being poisoned. It has to be something you can keep an eye on without it soaking up your time. The task can't be up high as they will fall off it. It can't be hot in any way or they will get heat exhaustion. It can't

involve anything sharp or they will ram it into their eye the second your back is turned. It can't be near water or they will dip it in it. The task can't be edible in any way or they will try to eat it. Most important, it can't have any long-term value or the gobshite will see to it that whatever fuck-up they make is irreversible. Keeping the gobshites you work with out of the way while still having them complete some form of task might require some thought and preparation, but it is well worth it.

6) *Explaining things to gobshites takes ages.* You need to allow time to explain things to the gobshites you work with. Gobshites never feel bad about delaying things excessively so that plans, instructions, details, timings, words and basic shit can be explained to them for a third and fourth time. The gobshite will rarely see that everyone else has grasped the plan. They drift off, they look out the window at the crucial moment of a fire safety protocol briefing or read a text message when you're telling them how to use the defibrillator. Is it worth it? Is it even worth the energy to explain that they will cut their fingers off if they try to retrieve grass from the underside of the lawnmower? Probably not. Based on the number of gobshite-related accidents, definitely not. But it can't do any harm and if there is a tribunal into how the company lost all that money or destroyed all those trees, you'll need to have it on record that you attempted to explain it to the gobshite responsible. (See point 4.)

7) *Gobshites move on.* It might feel like you're stuck working with this gobshite for the rest of your life, but you're not. Gobshites, in most cases, struggle to hold down jobs long term unless they work in government, state-run organisations or education. However upsetting the

gobshite in your office is, chances are they'll be gone soon enough. Think of it the way Andre Agassi used to play tennis. You don't need to hit winners every game. Sometimes you need to just let your opponent make their own mistakes. Keep giving the ball back to the gobshite. Let them reveal who they are. Sometimes the reason we defend the right to free speech is because it lets us see who exactly are the gobshites among us. Let the gobshite in your workplace finish their next dumb sentence. Let them pursue their idea. Just don't get labelled as the person who let them do it. (See point 3.)

8) *Gobshites tend to cancel each other out.* If you find there are two gobshites in your office or workplace, group them together. Isn't that dangerous? No. In a lot of cases the two gobshites will cancel each other out. Give a two-gobshite team responsibility for something you don't mind them making a complete mess of. The going-away party for Sean. At the end of the day, Sean doesn't want a going-away party. We are all going to go to the pub one way or another. Let the two office gobshites work on it. Their terrible ideas and awful work ethic will keep them out of the way and nothing will come of it. The key is finding the right task for them. (See point 5.)

9) *Never underestimate a gobshite's capacity to ruin things.* The gobshite finds a way to torpedo your best laid plans. It's not a skill they can put down on their CV. It's like a super close up power they are all born with. It doesn't matter what you do to try to subvert it, the gobshite is a slithery creature when it comes to finding a way to fuck things up. You might have given the gobshites you work with explicit directions to the street they need to go to. They will find a street of the same name in a different

town. You might have done 90 per cent of the painting they need to do for them. They will find a way to screw up the remaining 10 per cent in such a dramatic way that you need to start again. Never leave a gobshite unattended with work you know to be important, valuable or urgent. If the instructions are written on a piece of paper, that paper is gone. Despite all this, there are some jobs gobshites can complete successfully. There are recorded cases of gobshites successfully creating expense reports and even laying concrete. What these reports fail to mention is that the gobshites in both cases became instantly cocky and completely ruined the accounting software and pavement the following day.

10) *There is always an excuse with a gobshite co-worker.* No gobshite has ever said the words, 'This is all my fault.' You're far more likely to hear them say, 'You never explained it to me', 'I was on my break when it went on fire' or 'I have a sinus infection, how was I supposed to smell the gas?' The creative strength of gobshites lies in conjuring excuses for failed work, ballsed-up attempts and expensive disasters. Gobshites are like magicians when it comes to excuses. They can produce a rabbit from a hat and a half-baked sob story from up their sleeve in seconds. All they need is for the shit to hit the fan. (We will discuss this further in the upcoming chapter on how to spot when a gobshite is lying.) You therefore need to alert other members of staff to the gobshite's compulsion to magic up excuses for their fuck-ups. It needs to be on record for when they ruin something huge and you are brought up in front of management to explain what happened. Once everyone knows that the gobshite never sees themselves as the problem, it might even become funny. 'I was told bleach cleans everything!'

WHY DO GOBSHITES GET HIRED?

How do gobshites manage to wriggle their way into every company and organisation in the world? I bet if you think about it, there has been at least one gobshite in every business, club, institution and company you have ever worked for or dealt with. When you see people looking out the windows of buses and trains during rush hour, most of them are pondering how in the hell the incompetent gobshite in their workplace managed to get hired. Some of the commuters looking out the windows are wondering how that gobshite became the boss. Those smiling as they look out the windows are the gobshites. The recruitment industry invests millions each year in attempting to find new and more elaborate ways to screen out gobshites through selection processes. So why is it still happening so consistently? Why are gobshites beating to these roles skilled, well-mannered, self-aware applicants with no hygiene issues?

As mentioned in point 2, gobshites are unusually good in interviews and a lot of employers fail to check their references. But there is more to it than that. Gobshites get hired for a range of very simple reasons including the simplest one – gobshites are readily available. Gobshites are rarely busy, even though they should be doing any number of things. Taking care of their sick mother. Apologising to their ex. Sorting out their finances. Repairing the damage they did to their neighbour's fence when they stumbled over it drunk the previous evening. But they're not doing any of these things. Gobshites are consistently at a loose end, hovering around aimlessly like lemmings. Gobshites loiter. When a position opens up in a company or business, gobshites get the first box ticked because they can start right away. It's the same reason they get promotions. Others, too busy getting

Gobshite Time Spent in Work

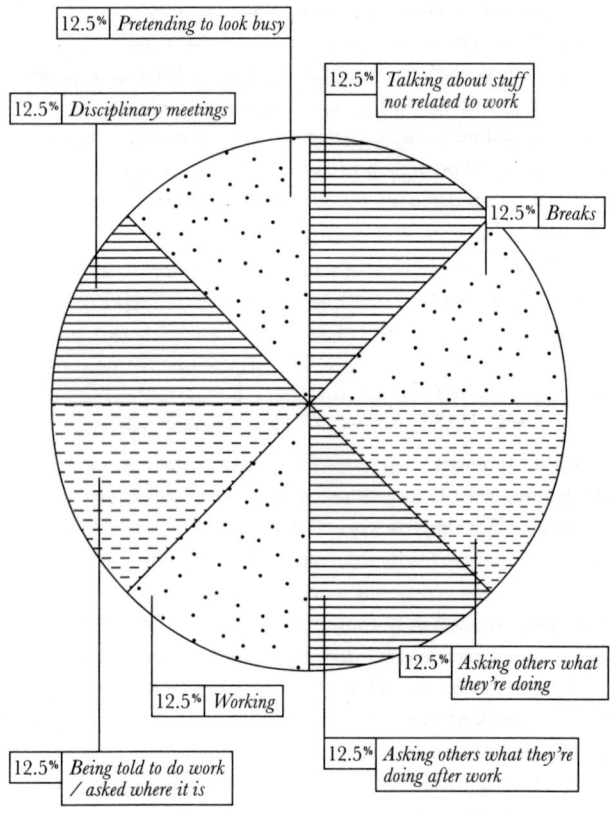

12.5% Pretending to look busy

12.5% Talking about stuff not related to work

12.5% Disciplinary meetings

12.5% Breaks

12.5% Asking others what they're doing

12.5% Working

12.5% Asking others what they're doing after work

12.5% Being told to do work / asked where it is

on with the work the gobshite has failed to do, fail to see the relevant message on the noticeboard or email and the gobshite swoops in.

Have you ever seen a fully fledged, card-carrying gobshite hired for a job you would have been perfect for? Chances are you were too busy working and the gobshite was the only applicant. You and I would call the hiring of this gobshite their dumb luck, but the gobshite knows on some level that showing up to as many parties as possible is the best way to get a girlfriend. As we have covered in a previous chapter, gobshites are doggedly persistent in spite of themselves. This is why so many gobshites win the lottery and blow their winnings. Gobshites will always remember to play the lottery (unless you send them down with your numbers written on a scrap of paper).

TODAY'S WORKFORCE ISSUES – 'WE JUST CAN'T GET THE STAFF!'

While economists have been bleating on about the lack of skilled employable individuals across the world, gobshites have been rubbing their hands together. Stores, coffee shops and small businesses have been forced to hire more and more gobshites in recent times because, they claim, the good people are just not applying for the jobs. It's left many people, including the good people who want jobs, scratching their heads. How are the gobshites soaking up all these roles and making our lives a misery? While this is happening, graduates with enough cop-on to know that you don't just blow on doughnuts that fall on the floor are left unable to pay their rent and forced to leave the country in the hope that there might be fewer gobshites abroad. (Spoiler alert: There's not. There's way more of them in England, America and France for some reason.)

Is it possible that the gobshites are running the asylum? Many believe that after years of the odd gobshite getting a few jobs here and there an inflection point has been reached. The first gobshites somehow managed to work their way up to management positions and are now enforcing a pro-gobshite recruiting strategy. These powerful gobshites may not even know they are doing this. They might just be positively discriminating in favour of the gobshites applying for jobs because they see themselves in the story of these applicants. Gobshite managers see a skilled, well-qualified applicant's CV and think, 'What a show-off!' The same manager looks positively on a gobshite CV that lists under achievements Xbox games the gobshite has completed, and under the category Sex the scrawled words, 'Not as much as I'd like'.

WHY DON'T NORMAL PEOPLE JUST FIRE ALL THE GOBSHITES WHEN THEY GET THE CHANCE?

Firing a gobshite is exceptionally hard. Just as breaking up with a gobshite is very tricky, it's never as straightforward as telling them it's over. Gobshites rarely get the message right away. If you intend to break up with or fire a gobshite, you need to bring a book of evidence with you. It needs to be made abundantly clear to the gobshite that they are not to come in tomorrow. Many gobshites still holding jobs today have been fired but continue to show up for work. They literally didn't get the memo. Gobshites are the reason America started the tradition of cleaning out a person's desk for them when they get fired. This was the only way to get it into the gobshite's head that tomorrow your stuff needs to be somewhere else. Gobshites get fired all the time. You just need to be ready for the push back against whatever you say (see handy diagram).

Gobshite Reactions to Being Fired

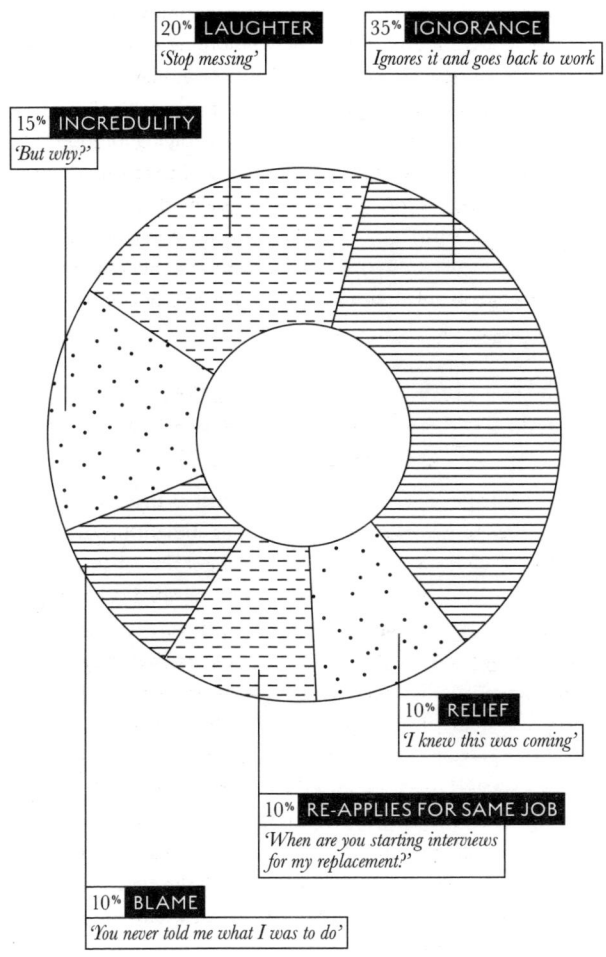

20% LAUGHTER
'Stop messing'

35% IGNORANCE
Ignores it and goes back to work

15% INCREDULITY
'But why?'

10% RELIEF
'I knew this was coming'

10% RE-APPLIES FOR SAME JOB
'When are you starting interviews for my replacement?'

10% BLAME
'You never told me what I was to do'

Workforce Gobshite Percentage

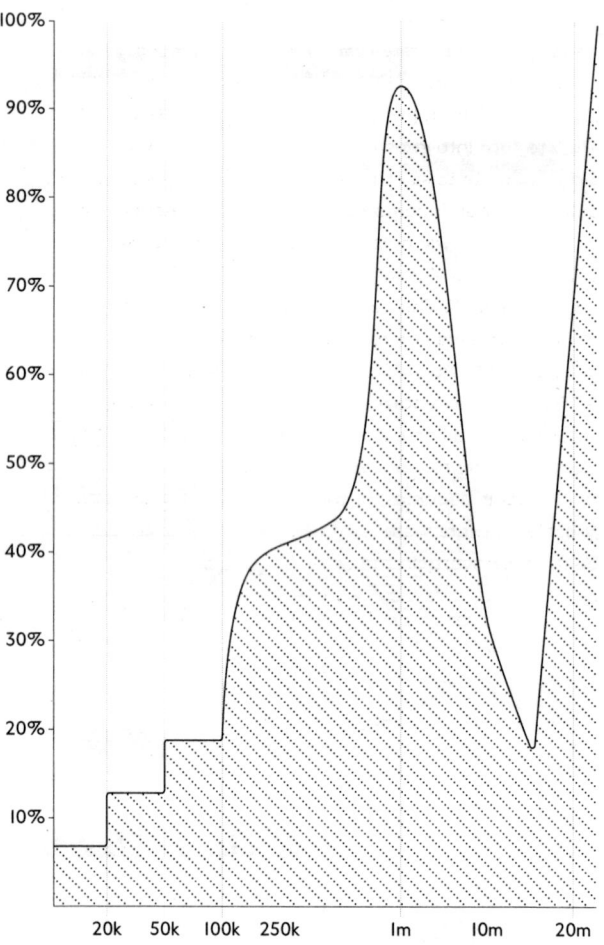

Earnings

HIGH-EARNING GOBSHITES

This diagram shows the percentage of gobshites versus annual income. As we can see, the percentage increases at a pretty predictable rate to a point. Every time a gobshite gets a promotion, more of their awful behavior seems justified in their minds. This is not to say that individuals become more likely to turn into gobshites the more money they earn. It's more accurate to say that gobshites tend to reveal their true colours as their income rises – see Kanye West or Conor McGregor. You will note the sudden rise in the percentage of gobshites earning more than €500K per annum and then a sudden fall off. This can be explained by the inability of gobshites to save and look after their wealth. The percentage continue to fall as we head into the 'mega rich' for the same reason. The percentage then shoots up once income rises above €200 million per annum. We call this 'Elon Musk Curve'. The more money a person has at this threshold, the harder it becomes for them not to behave like a total gobshite. If there were fewer gobshite billionaires there would be far less poverty in the world.

How to Spot When a Gobshite Is Lying

Nobody has more reasons to lie than a gobshite. When things inevitably go wrong, when they get caught or are forced to explain, the gobshite will immediately begin spouting sentences designed to cover their guilt. The only person who believes a gobshite in these situations is a fellow gobshite or their mother. We all need to be ready to spot these sentences like the piles of shite that they are. Once you realise that the gobshite you're dealing with is lying, it's important not to spook them. Don't leap to your feet and shout LIAR! If a gobshite shows their hand by saying any of the following sentences, you don't need to react with an accusation. You can have a bit of fun toying with them first instead. But always remember – the longer this goes on, the more likely it is that the gobshite will believe the lie they just told you.

SEVEN OF THE MOST COMMONLY USED GOBSHITE LIES

1. 'It was like that when I got here.'

Gobshites are not making notes of how things are on their arrival. They are barrelling through the world with a reckless abandon that often leads to them breaking fixtures, fittings, technology, protective railings, TV screens, fridge doors and anything that might require some sort of care and attention. 'It was like that when I got here' is a reflex sentence that leaves a gobshite's mouth when someone asks, 'What happened here?' or 'Who broke this?' The gobshite that says *it was like that when I got here* is so used to having to explain how they broke things, being forced to pay fines and issue embarrassing apologies that they fire this sentence out to nip any allegations in the bud. It usually has the opposite effect.

2. *'I heard about a guy who had a similar problem.'*

The first problem with this lie is that gobshites never really listen to anyone. So the idea that they were gathering eyewitness accounts from people who have experienced similar problems to the one they now find themselves in is clearly ridiculous. This sentence is a lie that gobshites use to convince others that the mess they have created is not that unusual and that nobody should be mad at them. To uncover the threadbare nature of this lie, one need only ask, 'Oh yeah, which guy? Give me his name.' Most gobshites will not have thought this through and will say, 'You wouldn't know him' or, 'It's a guy I used to work with.' Gobshite listening skills are so poor that any time a gobshite starts a sentence with the words 'I heard', you should be immediately dubious of whatever comes next.

3. *'There seemed to be a bit of confusion/ Nobody was clear on that.'*

The problem with this lie is that the gobshite believes it. The reality is nobody ever lets a gobshite do something without giving them a full explanation of the dangers involved. It's the reason why we all have to listen to the ridiculous in-flight tutorial on how to get out of the plane in the event of an emergency. Gobshites are the reason most safety tutorials were created. When a gobshite says 'Nobody explained that to me', they're really saying 'I didn't listen when that was being explained to me' or 'Someone tried to explain it to me but I was busy wondering why my veins are blue but my blood is red.' A lot of the time a gobshite will say 'Nobody explained that to me' to the person who explained that to them. Stay calm and remember to film your explanation and back it up to some sort of online cloud resource while holding a copy of today's newspaper.

4. *'I tried but they wouldn't let me. I swear.'*

The dead giveaway here is the 'I swear'. Any time a gobshite says 'I swear', whatever previous statement he is referring to ceases to be considered valid. 'I let the dog out last night, I swear.' 'That money was just resting in my account, I SWEAR.' 'Even the teachers admitted that I was the best, I SWEAR.' The blaming of others is another go-to lie of the gobshite that is frequently followed by 'I swear'. There's always someone who wouldn't give them a chance. Someone who wrestled them to the floor and wouldn't let them wash their hands after using the toilet. Another person who was gunning for their downfall. Because as we all know by now, the gobshite, in their own mind, is being given a very hard time by the world.

5. *'I was just thinking the same thing.'*

When a gobshite tells you they have had the same idea as you, they don't mean that, previous to this conversation and independently of you, they had the exact same thought. They mean that they thought of your idea as you were explaining the idea to them. As in – they heard what you said and understood it. Gobshites are very confused on this issue. They believe their own bullshit when it comes to idea conception. Never try to explain a valuable new idea to a gobshite. You run the risk of them co-opting the idea as their own, or, worse, believing sincerely that they co-created the idea simply because it was explained to them. Here's an example.

Mark: 'I was thinking we should organise a surprise party for Mom and Dad to celebrate their wedding anniversary.'

Gobshite: 'I was just thinking the same thing. Hey everyone, Mark and I have just had a brilliant idea.'

This gobshite has no plan or idea for a surprise party. He was, up until moments ago, blissfully unaware of his parents' upcoming anniversary. Now that Mark has explained his idea to him, he has confused his realisation that his parents' wedding anniversary is upcoming with actually having the idea to celebrate it with a surprise party. Both feelings are similar to the gobshite. It's like when a person, unbeknown to themselves, spills a warm liquid in their lap. For a brief moment they can't tell if they have pissed themselves. Having ideas is the same kind of sensation for a gobshite. They have no control over them. Occasionally they are credited with a good idea but in their heart they know that, like the time they pissed their pants on that rollercoaster, it just happened. It wasn't intentional. If a gobshite says 'I was just thinking the same thing', they mean 'I am now thinking of the thing you just told me about.'

6. *'Will you relax? I definitely checked it before I left.'*

All gobshites live life flying by the seat of their pants. Just as a gobshite would simply never read a set of instructions, neither would it ever occur to them to check whether or not something has been done. If a gobshite assures you that something has been checked, they are definitely lying to you. They may run from the room directly after saying this. If you're lucky, they are racing off to double check on the thing. If you're unlucky, they are fleeing the area because they know whatever disaster is about to unfold will be blamed on them.

7. 'It will be safe with me.'

This is perhaps the most dangerous promise you can believe from the mouth of any gobshite. Nothing is ever truly safe in the hands of a gobshite. Parents of gobshites know this implicitly. You can't leave cotton wool in the care of a gobshite. They will attempt to swallow it. Should a gobshite ever wind up in a position of caregiver or security guard, disaster is not far away. But surely I can leave my lunch with a gobshite while I go to the toilet in a restaurant? 'No' is the simple answer here. There is a slim chance your food will still be there when you return but it is highly unlikely. They will either eat some of it, pour salt on it 'for the craic' or allow the server to take it away. In this situation, you are better off bringing your plate with you and eating the remainder of your meal in the bathroom or when you return. Many gobshites know that they are not to be trusted with anything, so it is rare enough for them to volunteer and utter the lie, 'it will be safe with me'.

ALCOHOL'S IMPACT ON LYING GOBSHITES

As mentioned in a previous chapter, the biggest blind spot among all gobshites, aside from any understanding of health, safety and manners, concerns respect for the intelligence of others. Day to day the gobshite walks around thinking nobody knows about their shoddily repaired car, second-hand suit or the lies they continue to tell. They simply can't countenance the idea that their attempts to be cunning are as transparent as those white swimming togs they thought were a great bargain in that shop in Spain. Alcohol gives all gobshites an even greater sense of superiority. Call it Dutch courage, call it similarly inebriated people being more willing to listen to them – once a gobshite has alcohol in their system, the cock and bull stories just fly out of their empty heads. A gobshite won't lie about certain things when sober but once drunk all limits go out the window. Jobs they once had – 'I used to work for a Formula One team, you know.' People they dated: 'You know your one off *Buffy the Vampire Slayer*? Well, she was filming in Dublin and I was working in the hotel she was staying at ...' The stories will get more and more elaborate the more they drink. You can either nod along and enjoy these made-up stories for the fiction they are or challenge them on the details. 'So, Sarah Michelle Gellar laid eyes on you and decided to leave Ryan Phillippe in that moment? You?' The gobshite will always double down on any drunken lie they tell. So you really are entering a world of pain. And, as mentioned in a previous chapter, arguing with a gobshite can cause you to be dragged down to their level. Be aware that if you're seen arguing with a known gobshite over whether he shifted Buffy the Vampire Slayer, it may be hard for a member of the general public to differentiate between you and the gobshite. As the old saying goes, 'Never argue with a gobshite. They will drag you down to their level and beat you with experience.'

Gobshites in Politics

BORIS JOHNSON

Boris falls into the category of that gobshite who gets away with murder because some people find him funny. There is no difference between Johnson shrugging off the hames he made of the lockdowns in the UK and the lad in your office who manages to make his catastrophic Christmas party booking a great story he gets to tell to clients. The nickname Bojo is further evidence of how a gobshite like this seems to skate above the trail of destruction he leaves behind him. When presented with his ineptitude by the press, people in the street, his many girlfriends or the Commons Privileges Committee, Boris had a way to gobshite his way out of trouble. His knack for deflecting attention or saying something so absurd the issue became irrelevant was his superpower. Will we ever see his like again? I wouldn't hold hold your breath.

NIGEL FARAGE

Some question whether this man is a gobshite or just a complete and utter spanner. The subtle differences between the two will be discussed in detail later in this book. Nigel is definitely a mouthpiece who enjoys winding others up. If he is a gobshite, he is the kind of gobshite who thinks good conversation means disagreeing with the general consensus. This kind of gobshite in politics is particularly dangerous because they spout opinions as facts. Opinions that are for the most part offensive, hurtful and designed to agitate minorities don't bother them whatsoever. They view themselves as courageous for voicing opinions others won't. This kind of political figure sees themselves as a crusader for free speech rather than an attention-seeking gobshite devoid of empathy. From his 'Up the Ra' Cameo debacle to losing an election to a dolphin in 2010 to spewing nonsense throughout the Brexit referendum, Nigel wrote the book on how to be a modern political gobshite. He calls it his autobiography. *Flying Free.*

PRESIDENT GEORGE W. BUSH

'They misunderestimated me.' George was one of those easily led gobshites who somehow found himself at the steering wheel of a vehicle he had no clue how to drive. That vehicle was the United States of America and the lads egging him on to do doughnuts in the car park were Dick Cheney and Donald Rumsfeld. George should never have been president. He knew it, Al Gore knew it, but most of all, Cheney knew it. As George's vice president, Cheney played upon the president's lack of self-belief and used his influence to push through some brutal decisions that would have a devastating impact on the world. Only a gobshite would allow themselves to be pushed around in this way while holding the highest office in the land. He could have fired Cheney at any moment but he felt indebted to him in some weird way. Then there were the verbal screw-ups. It's almost cute to think about the silly things Bush used to say when compared to the bananas stuff that has been the norm since 2016. But George really came out with dozens of classic lines any gobshite would be proud of. 'Families is where nations find hope, where wings take dream.' 'Our enemies are innovative and resourceful, and so are we. They never stop thinking about new ways to harm our country and our people, and neither do we.'

KAROLINE LEAVITT

In 2024, after years of just being a big lick, Karoline was ordained as a fully qualified gobshite when she accepted the job as White House press secretary. Her role as chief gobshite translator and hype man for Donald Trump has suited her down to the ground. Her fluency in the language of the gobshite has perfectly positioned her to bang on about how well things are going while the shit is clearly hitting the fan. Where previous press secretaries have struggled to make sense of the nonsense that has emerged from the desk at the Oval Office, Karoline has had no such problems. Her bewildering fights with journalists over their attempts to ask simple questions have made her the gobshite flavour of the month with the president. Say what you like about Trumplestiltskin, he knows gobshites when he sees them. In the current crop of gobshites and yes men he has chosen to surround himself with, Karoline is top of the heap. Chances are by the time you read this she will have been fired and will have a book out explaining why she's not actually a gobshite.

GEORGE SANTOS

George is that gobshite who gets caught doing something so obviously wrong that the main question the authorities have for him is 'How did you think you were going to get away with it?' The answer is these gobshites never think that far ahead. Santos admitted to deceiving donors and stealing the identities of nearly a dozen people, including his family members, to fund his political campaign. The IRS summarised the charges that were eventually brought against him as follows: 'George Santos lied to his constituents, cheated his supporters and quite simply made a mockery of his position in public office.' The gobshite who is oblivious to the consequences of their actions is among the most infuriating – that's our George. Right up to the point where he was sentenced to seven years in prison, George never seemed to get that what he did was wrong. Santos's behaviour was so absurd and off the wall, we are guaranteed a Netflix documentary about him in the future. His ruptured relationship with the truth resulted in him concocting some of the most spectacularly stupid lies ever to leave the mouth of any gobshite in political history. For starters, he said he had been a star volleyball player at a college he never attended. He said his mother had been working in her office in the World Trade Center on the morning of 11 September 2001 when she wasn't in the country. He bragged about producing *Spider-Man: Turn Off the Dark*, the biggest Broadway flop of the modern era. Just like your gobshite cousin who wound up in prison, there was always an excuse and always a reason as to why George Santos was not the problem.

BORIS YELTSIN

Another Boris who somehow clambered his way to power by being up for pints whenever anyone offered. Yeltsin took the reins from Mikhail Gorbachev amidst a coup surrounded by other military gobshites who didn't like the country's reforms. Yeltsin went on to create even greater reforms but because he was a man of the people, he got away with utter madness. He was a party animal by all accounts or 'fond of the gargle', as your uncle might say. Or drunk most of the time, as a doctor might say. He once failed to get off his plane in Dublin Airport due to being hungover. That would be a relatable story if the Irish Taoiseach and press core were not waiting on the tarmac to meet him at the steps of the aircraft. Eventually it became obvious that this gobshite wasn't going to come down the steps and everyone went home in a taxi.

That really is the tip of the iceberg when it comes to Boris Yeltsin's gobshite résumé. Most high-grade gobshites cause an accident in the early years. Usually they don't receive the punishment they deserve and become emboldened in their gobshite ways. Young Boris lost the index finger and thumb of his left hand as a boy while attempting to play a prank with some grenades he had stolen. That should have been a sign that this was not a man you could leave in charge of a towel at the beach, never mind a country with the arsenal of Russia. His final act as leader was to chose Vladimir Putin as his successor. Just like that gobshite who ruined the school tour so badly that nobody got to go on one ever again, this was a move the world has been paying the price for ever since.

A CONCERNING TREND

Just like sea swimming and MMA, politics has always attracted a certain amount of gobshites. In this diagram we can see the baseline level of gobshites in politics was far lower from 1930 to 1970. There is then a steady rise as more and more gobshites viewed politics as a cushy number. The dip from 2000 to 2015 can be explained by the global economy and terrorism issues faced during this period. This sounded too much like hard work to most gobshites. Since 2016 gobshites have dominated global politics and this worrying trend looks set to continue.

Number of Gobshites in Politics

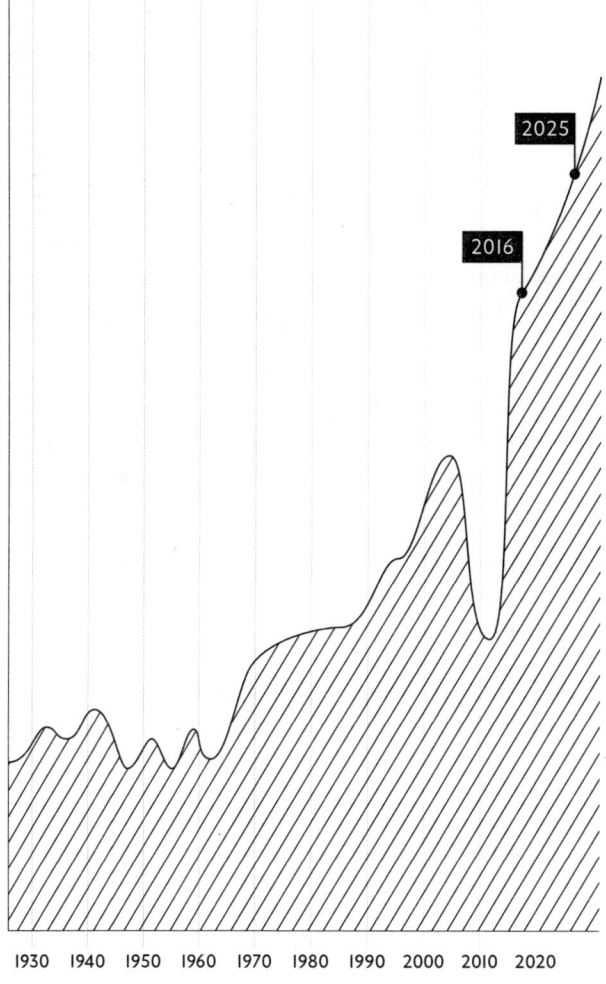

24

Can Animals Be Gobshites?

It's normal to hear people refer to animals as gobshites. 'Don't mind my dog. He's a real gobshite when I take him for walks.' 'I called my cat Seamus because he's such a gobshite I thought the name suited him.' 'The horse refused to jump the fence. Some days he's a total gobshite. I don't know what we're going to do with him.' But are these animals actual gobshites or are we projecting human characteristics onto them in the same way we might say a goat is cunning? Is the goat really cunning or is he just trying his best to figure out a way to stay alive? Nibbling through the shopping that was left at the front door isn't cunning, it's slightly opportunistic. The goat is far more of a little bollocks than he is an evil genius.

Zoologists haven't bothered their arses looking into whether animals can be gobshites. They also refuse to reply when you send them emails on the subject. Some of them hang up the phone on you when you call them to ask if it's possible that an animal could be a gobshite. You can call them back but eventually they block the number or, worse still, tell other zoologists not to answer the phone to you. At least that's what I think happened. It appears the zoologist community is as closed-minded as it is tightly knit. They definitely have a WhatsApp group chat. One can only imagine how fucking boring that group chat is, but let's get back to the question. Can animals be gobshites? Undoubtedly, the answer is yes. How can I say this with such certainty? One word: Valentine.

VALENTINE THE DOG

Valentine is a dog I have lived with for the last three years. That sounds like he's my flatmate but our living situation is far worse. Valentine is owned by the couple I live with. And as such I can't ask him to move out or have a flat meeting where we go over the rules of living with each other. At such a meeting I would tell Valentine that I think it is unacceptable to randomly start shouting at the top of his lungs throughout the day. I would say that pissing in the house is unhygienic and upsetting, especially when moments earlier he had gone outside claiming to need a piss. I would say to Valentine at our flat meeting that he will have to move out if he continues to spread his food all around the floor. But such a meeting can never occur because Valentine is a little white gobshite dog who is beloved by his owners. Aside from them, anyone who has ever come into contact with this dog is left in no doubt that gobshite animals exist.

But are dogs innocent? When they arrive into the world, yes. Dogs such as Valentine, when they are born, know no better than to bark at open cupboards, the sound of a set of keys in the door or the sky. But when a dog is eight years old and has had the rules of the house explained to him on a daily basis each and every day of that eight-year period and is still so shocked and irritated by someone sitting down in a chair that he barks his brains out for the rest of the evening – that's a gobshite. Some may argue that Valentine is merely an anxious animal who needs routine, stability, affection and structure to let him know that everything is okay and that there is no need to piss everywhere every single day and bark until you get sick every evening. Those who argue this have never met Valentine. Valentine has received all of those things and still insists on being a thoroughbred gobshite every day of his existence. Not convinced? Still think all dogs are by their nature kind, gentle, intuitive darlings that just need love? Consider these things I have observed in the last eight years.

- Valentine does not drink water by lapping it into his mouth using his long doggy tongue. Valentine jabs at his water bowl with his paw until the water splashes up into the air. He then runs beneath the splash with his mouth open in an attempt to catch the water in his mouth. This understandably creates a colossal mess but that is how Valentine likes it.

- Valentine likes to dig. Not digging in the grass or muck like a normal dog. Not to bury a bone. Valentine has absolutely no interest in bones. No, Valentine enjoys digging at the tiles in the floor in the utility room where he sleeps. Despite the fact that he never makes any indentation or progress, despite the fact that he never produces a hole through his feverish digging motion, Valentine will while away a couple of hours out of each day digging and going nowhere.

- Most dogs cock their leg when going for a whizz. It's a doggy tradition. Nobody has to show them to do this, dogs just know. For maximum coverage and minimum splash-back, best practice for a dog when pissing is to cock the hind leg on either side to 75 degrees or more and let fly on your piss target. Valentine never got the memo. On the rare occasion when Valentine actually

Daily Breakdown of Valentine's Mind

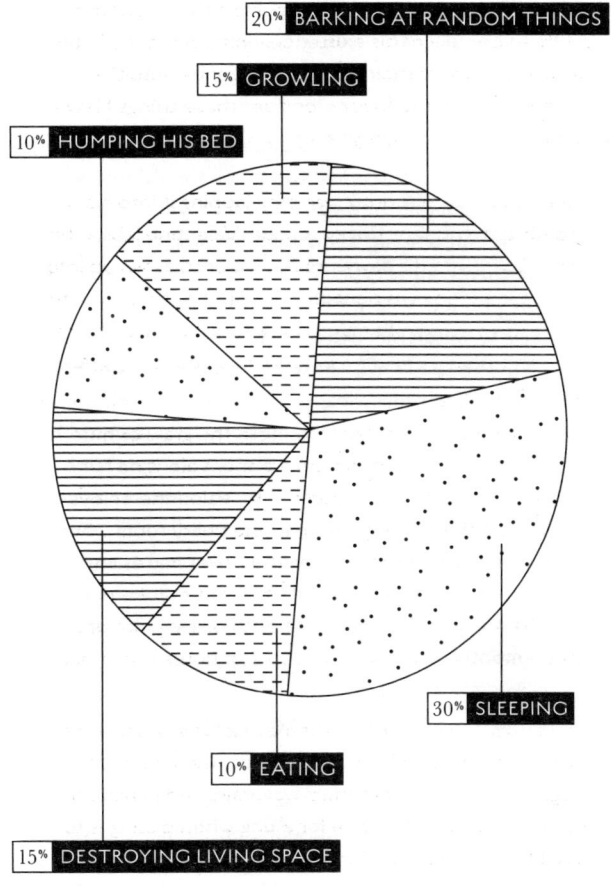

20% BARKING AT RANDOM THINGS

15% GROWLING

10% HUMPING HIS BED

30% SLEEPING

10% EATING

15% DESTROYING LIVING SPACE

whizzes outside, he does so all over himself. The leg cock is not something he partakes in. Other dogs look at him while he destroys his coat with his own urine the way we humans look at gobshites who can't navigate revolving doors. The expression on these dogs' faces has to be seen to be believed. These dogs might not know what a gobshite is but when they look at Valentine, that's the closest they can get.

- Occasionally Valentine will go rogue. Like all gobshites, sometimes the world is just too much for Valentine. You know that gobshite you knew from years ago who wandered off one night and near speared himself climbing over some gates? Valentine does that too. The person who lets Valentine out to piss on himself before bed has to watch him like a hawk or he will disappear. Twice in the last 12 months when the person watching him has turned their back, Valentine has taken off like a hostage fleeing his captors. Nobody knows where he is going when he does this. I'm pretty sure Valentine doesn't know where he is going when he makes a break for the border. During his most recent wild adventure he got mauled by two wolfhounds in a neighbouring garden. The injuries he sustained were not sufficiently life-altering for him not to attempt the same bullshit three months later.

CAN GOBSHITE DOGS EXPLAIN GOBSHITE WEDDINGS?

And yet despite all of this, I and many others still feel affection, even love, for Valentine the dog. It makes absolute no logical sense. This animal melts everyone's head. He is the cause of so much anxiety and pain. And yet we love him. Could this simple animal explain how human gobshites find love? 'Did you hear Sarah is getting married to Paul?' 'Not Paul! Why in God's name would a nice girl like Sarah marry a gobshite like that lad? What does she see in him at all?' It's a very common conversation. Many parents have had sleepless nights over the union of a gobshite and a non-gobshite, or even of two gobshites. Is the shambles somehow attractive? Perhaps gobshite dogs are our only way of ever understanding why a man named Jim, who can't hold down a few pints never mind a job, could marry your lovely cousin Clare.

While Valentine the dog and dogs like him (see the motion picture *Marley & Me*) are definitive proof that an animal can exhibit all the characteristics of a gobshite, the question remains: is there a species of animal that is predominantly gobshite? While our zoologist friends might not want to comment, I think the argument can be made for one species of animal.

HORSES ARE GOBSHITES

Most horses are gobshites. Horse lovers tell themselves that horses are complex creatures, highly sensitive to the emotions of others, honest to a fault, willing to transport their master at high speed across all terrain in all weather conditions. The reality is that horses, with the very odd exception (Seabiscuit, Black Beauty, the Black Stallion and that horse Gandalf rode in *The Lord of the Rings*) are all gobshites of the worst kind. Horses, like gobshites, can't ever be trusted. No horse trainer or equestrian professional would ever recommend you walk behind a horse. They shout at you if you do it. 'Jesus Christ, don't walk behind the filly, Jarlath! She's likely to take the fucking head off you with a kick.' What kind of a relationship is that? Is there any other tamed animal in the world that garners this much love and affection that would in a heartbeat attempt to maim and kill its owner? You can't really blame horses for this one, though.

Owners and horse lovers are often good, smart people in other sectors of their lives, holding down jobs, raising children or even driving cars. But when it comes to their beloved horses, they are completely and utterly deluded. They will tell you their horse loves them. They may even tell you their horse has a good sense of humour or a great sense of adventure. Let there be no mistake, horses fucking hate us. All of us. Horses look at humans the way Egyptian slaves looked at the pharaoh. 'Just give me the chance.' 'Walk behind me once and I'll nail some shoes on you, bitch.' You can't blame the horse for thinking we are dicks. We are monsters to them. To ride them we 'break' them. Literally break their spirit. Horses that can't be broken are demonised by horse people. 'That horse is too wilful.' That horse knows well what you're trying to do to him. He's the only one with a bit of common sense. Those horses, the ones the stud farmers give up on, are, from what I can see, the only non-gobshite horses in the world today.

But even without the whole nailing of shoes to their feet and insisting they let us ride them for absolutely no reason other than 'fun', horses are gobshites even when they're wild. Wild horses are used as a bar for idiotic behaviour. 'The guy took off like a wild horse.' 'Your man ran through the electric fence like a wild horse.' It could be argued that wild horses are this highly strung because they are worried someone might try to capture them and nail shoes to their feet. But take a look at cows. Cows know about other cows being slaughtered. You can see it in their adorable eyes under their cute little fringes. The cows are well aware that shit is about to go south for them very soon and yet they are completely chill about it. They are in a permanent state of shrugging. While horses, after centuries of knowing their lot in life, have not for a second relaxed into being ridden around in circles by tiny men in glorified clown suits. It's been this way for literally hundreds of years. Even domesticated birds have settled down to the idea that life in a cage with all the seed you can eat ain't so bad. Not horses. Horses get treated like royalty if they run fast. But that's all we are asking of them. You like running, right, guys? You're running around constantly in the wild. Well, how about you run around in a circle for us and in return we will set you up to have sex with another fast horse for the rest of your life? These gobshites are like, no. I don't want to run now. I am not going to run fast for you. I'm going to try to kill you. Now that's a gobshite.

CAN GOBSHITES KEEP PETS?

Gobshites can certainly own animals, but they rarely keep them for an extended period. The RSPCA estimates that 80 per cent of all dogs in shelters are the puppies of gobshites. In reality, a gobshite never really gets a dog in the same way a toddler never gets a harmonica. When a gobshite buys a dog it becomes the burden of everyone around them.

How Gobshites React in Emergencies

There's a big difference between a person who panics during an emergency and a gobshite in an emergency who makes things a lot worse. It's normal to feel anxious and stressed when the shit hits the fan. The shit should never have been placed that close to the fan to start with. There's shit flying everywhere now and the longer it goes on the more difficult the clean-up becomes. Most of us get better at coping with emergencies the more experience we have of them. The more we see the benefit of keeping a cool head when the kitchen nearly goes on fire, the more likely we are to stay calm the next time it happens. Most of us widen out that learning to other situations like someone choking. The first thing any emergency worker will tell you is to stay calm. Once we have done it once, we see it as the reason we were able to navigate out of trouble.

The gobshite does not see it that way. Gobshites have a very limited range of reactions during an emergency. None of them involves staying calm.

SHOUTING

'Oh God', 'Oh fuck' and 'What the fuck' are the three phrases you will most commonly hear a gobshite shouting at the scene of an accident. Gobshites will neglect all other actions that might help in favour of shouting 'Oh God', 'Oh fuck' or 'What the fuck' over and over again. There could be a functioning power hose in their hands at the scene of a fire and the gobshite will focus all their energy on shouting one or all of these phrases over and over again, rather than turning on the hose to douse the flames. If you arrive at the scene of an emergency and need to quickly identify who not to speak to about what has taken place, just look for the gobshite shouting 'Oh fuck', 'Oh Jesus' or 'What the fuck'. Even if you were to ask this gobshite how you can help or what happened, the chances are they will simply repeat the above phrases while clutching their head. This applies to workplace emergencies such as deleting crucial files, family emergencies like leaving an elderly relative unattended or personal emergencies such as transferring money to the bank account of a person claiming to be a foreign prince. The gobshite may devote the first few crucial minutes to repeating these phrases rather than attempting to do anything else.

STATING THE OBVIOUS

'She's choking.' You might hear a gobshite at the scene of an emergency stating the blindingly obvious without doing anything about it. Shouting 'She's choking' while a person gasps for air or begs to have someone perform the Heimlich manoeuvre is a great example of this. Telling everyone else what's going on is how a gobshite copes with crises in their own life, so they are simply applying that to this situation. They don't see themselves as the solution or even part of the solution to any problem. If someone is choking, if a baby is eating paint or if a driverless car is rolling down a hill, the gobshite believes that the best way they can lend help is by telling everyone what is happening. This is not raising the alarm. They would never run to tell a medic or competent person. Gobshites are just saying what they see. 'Oh fuck, oh fuck, oh fuck, the door is about to come off that thing' is what you might hear a gobshite say while standing within arms' reach of the thing.

RUNNING AROUND

Running to get help is often the most important thing you can do in an emergency situation. Having the 'cop-on' to go get the lifeguard, fire brigade or parents is not something you will ever see a gobshite do in an emergency. You're more than likely to see a gobshite running back and forth. During the investigation into why a disaster took place, it may emerge that if the gobshite involved had run to get help the whole thing could have been avoided. A gobshite who has been involved in such an investigation will apply that learning at the wrong time. Rather than taking evasive action at the scene, runner gobshites will run from the thing that needs help, fearing they will be blamed for not getting help again.

ASKING THE WORST QUESTIONS

'Is he going to die?' 'Why didn't you lock the gate?' 'Do you think we will still be going to the cinema later on?' 'Can I still have a go on the quad bike once he's in the ambulance?' Never underestimate a gobshite's capacity to ask the absolute wrong question during an emergency. If you can think of the most inappropriate and poorly timed question to come out with when all hell is breaking loose, a gobshite will have thought of it before you and blurted it out to the very last person who should hear it. 'He was going too fast, wasn't he?' 'I know he's really hurt but didn't it look so cool when he was flying through the air?' You can't react to the gobshite in these situations. You need to get someone to shepherd them away from the scene or they might get punched in the face by one or more people. Gobshite-induced fights are a common occurrence after traffic collisions for this very reason. 'Was I meant to stop back there?'

MOVING ON TOO QUICKLY

Calamitous situations, hair-raising events, disasters and emergencies are a daily occurrence for all gobshites. It's the main reason why they seem to move on from them so quickly. The house might still be on fire, the ambulance may not have arrived, people might still be missing – the gobshite might be already playing Angry Birds on their phone or asking you to watch a 'really funny' video on TikTok. This drives regular people absolutely crazy. Gobshites are completely puzzled by the anger. As far as they are concerned the child is missing, and there's nothing wrong with having a bit of laugh while trying to find him. If you find yourself in an emergency with a gobshite, like a car being stolen, you need to prepare yourself for the gobshite actually forgetting that the car has been stolen shortly after you visit the police station. They may even ask you where your car is. Or they might suggest driving to the cinema that evening to take your mind off what happened.

MAKING JOKES ABOUT THE EMERGENCY

Gobshites always think that people involved in terrible events or emergencies need to lighten up. This is usually because they have made a poorly timed joke too soon after the terrible event or emergency and been told to shut the fuck up. All gobshites believe that you have to laugh about these things, especially when they are responsible for the disaster that is currently unfolding. They may turn to you while you're attempting to reason with the police over the drunken vandalism your gobshite engaged in the night before and say, 'The mad thing is I did honours art for the Leaving Certificate!' You might have just buried the dog they ran over and the gobshite might quip, 'The next dog you get needs to be a watch dog.' If you express any frustration, if you do anything other than laugh and clap them on the back for being so much fun in the face of such sadness, they will become instantly offended and emotionally wounded. 'I'm only trying to look at the bright side of all this. You're so serious.'

HAVING NO CONCEPT OF THEIR PLACE OR ROLE

Just as the gobshite has no sense of timing with jokes during a time of loss, they have absolutely no fucking clue of where they fit in relation to emergencies or events that require serious or urgent actions. At the scene of an accident, they might ask an attractive paramedic on a date. At the scene of a police investigation, they might push past the victims to see if they can get a better look at things. This is especially the case if they caused the emergency or calamity before them. They may even forget that they were the one who fed all the chocolate to the dog whose stomach is now being pumped. They may even tell the vet that you really can't feed dogs chocolate.

HONING IN ON THEIR VERY LIMITED ROLE IN RESOLVING THE SITUATION

'I was the one who said we needed to call the ambulance.' 'Nobody would have known about the flood if it wasn't for me.' 'The policeman thanked me for letting him in when he arrived.' 'I think the tea I made really settled everyone down.' 'It was lucky I was here or there would have been no way to get in to stop the fire I started.' The rewriting of history is a key project in most gobshites' lives. They spend a lot of their time trying to convince the world that they were not the root cause of any difficulty encountered either by themselves or those near them. 'Apparently the wires were faulty. The electrician said these would need to be replaced in 10 years no matter what we did. In a way I did the company a favour by sawing through them.' You might think it would be pointless to set a gobshite straight on this stuff. Surely a gobshite is going to believe whatever he wants to believe – there is no point whatsoever in telling them out loud that the wires would have been fine for another 10 years if they hadn't cut them. Or that the baby didn't need a check-up anyway. Or that the car doesn't look better with a new bumper. Or that the hotel wasn't a shithole and that it would have been nice to have the option to stay there in years to come. And you would be right. There is no point in telling them any of this. And yet somehow we feel the urge to do it anyway.

WE ALL NEED A GOBSHITE EMERGENCY EMERGENCY PLAN

It's not enough to have a plan in the case of an emergency. You need a plan for the gobshites in your life in the case of an emergency. It can be as simple as 'run and hide up a tree until it all boils over.' The important thing to understand is that the gobshites in your workplace, family or organisation will not adhere to the regular emergency plan. There needs to be a gobshite-specific plan that takes into account their inability to follow directions and their propensity to panic and leave a burning building, locking the doors behind them as they go.

These are some things to remember when designing your plan for your gobshite.

1) **Keep it Simple** – I mean small words. Basic language they can remember in the moment. Turn off the power, get Dad, phone Mum. Anything beyond this is going to go over their heads or, worse, lead to questions in the moment. 'I know you said to call Dad at work if something happens with the gas in the house but he wasn't at work so I just said I'd wait until he got home. I was just trying to stick to the emergency plan that *you* gave me.'

2) **Make it Rhyme** – Gobshites have a greater chance of remembering what to do in a emergency if they have some sort of rhyming device to rely upon. 'If things go boom, get out of the room.' 'If things are going on fire and the situation is dire, don't stop and stare, don't run up the stairs.' The rhyme needs to be explicit and specific or they will lose focus or, worse, try to come up with their own ideas.

3) **Print it** – The plan needs to be visible somewhere. The gobshite won't read it if they have to find it first. This is why instruction booklets are completely wasted on gobshites. Hang your big red sign with the plan on it right in the place where you think the disaster might occurs – the stove, the garage, the fuse box, under the kitchen sink.

The sad part is there is every chance that a gobshite might ignore an emergency plan that is tattooed onto the inside of their eyelids. You can scream the plan at them every morning before they leave the house and the gobshite will eventually zone it out or completely forget it in minutes. The fact they nod and say 'fine, okay, I get it' is no guarantee a gobshite has heard what you said. So good luck out there. It's a very dangerous world, made all the more dangerous by the constant presence of gobshites in our lives.

26

If He Isn't a Gobshite, What Is He?

Perhaps you have a brother who raised a few red flags but after reading this book you realise he's not in fact a gobshite. He might be thick when it comes to owning a pet, he might be incompetent when it comes to booking flights and he might regularly get thrown out of nightclubs and weddings; but he might not be the type of person who would be accepted into the gobshite union should such a union exist – and we all hope it doesn't. But what is he, then? If he's not a gobshite there's a range of sub-categories of fool this person might fit into. These people are not as dangerous as a gobshite but can at times drive you to drink. Examine the sub-categories below and be conscious that the person who is melting your head could fall into multiple categories.

HE COULD BE A KNOB

A knob is an individual who enjoys causing difficulty for others. Knobs report people to the tax man, thus forcing them to do a tax audit. Knobs insist on making their own way to the airport when getting a taxi together would save everyone money. Knobs, like gobshites, think they are smarter than other people. Unlike gobshites, they won't accept when they're proven to be wrong. A gobshite will attempt to fix your car if he puts a dint in it. A knob will pretend the dint was there before he drove the car. Knobs are underhanded in a way that enrages others because they assume others can't see through their bullshit. That's the true stupidity of a knob. While the knob thinks nobody noticed they didn't pay their share of the meal, the gobshite pays his share and then leaves his wallet in the taxi home from the restaurant.

HE COULD BE A DOPE

Gobshites are often confused with dopes because they share key characteristics and often wind up looking to you for help. A dope is significantly dumber than a gobshite in most cases. Gobshites can bungle their way through the education system and job interviews, gain employment and then through their lack of common sense make life a misery for everyone working alongside them. Dopes struggle to get the basics right. Being a complete dope means filling in forms is a challenge. Dopes can be told how and when to book the tickets, and still somehow manage to book too few tickets for the wrong show in the wrong city. A gobshite will make your life more difficult. A dope will force you to leave work to come and get them. If you realise that the person you love is not a gobshite but in fact a dope then you do not need this book. You need to change your name and move to a different country to start a better life.

HE COULD BE A SPANNER

Spanners are much less dangerous than gobshites, knobs or dopes. But spanners have a malevolent streak that makes them obnoxious to deal with. They are drawn to the teaching, bus driving and refereeing professions. They enjoy telling people when things are unavailable. When you lose your wallet, a spanner will tell you, 'You should have been more careful.'

HE COULD BE A BELLEND

Bellend is British term that was coined to describe people who upset plans, events, occasions and public gatherings. 'Oh, for God's sake, some bellend is running around the pitch stark bollock naked!' Bellends demand attention, and are often arrested, but they are not necessarily full-blown gobshites. Bellends might seem harmless but they are not. Bellends are often entrusted with responsibilities in the workplace, such as the whip-around for a going-away do. They will then usually lose or drink the money collected. In 2016, Britain allowed a bellend named David Cameron to be prime minister in spite of widespread rumours regarding his bellend behaviour in university – there were confirmed sightings of Cameron putting his willy in the mouth of a pig at a banquet with other bellends. Needless to say his reign as leader didn't work out well.

HE COULD BE A DICK

Dicks are a global problem. They are far more common than gobshites because everyone can be a bit of a dick sometimes. Everyone. Yes, even you. Being a dick is an act more than an identity. 'When we tried to check out just after midday, the receptionist was a dick about it. In the end the manager was a dick too and charged us for an extra night in the hotel.' Dickish behaviour is rampant in certain industries and workplaces. Parking attendants are paid to be dicks to people. Is it possible for a person to become a dick if they engage in dickish behaviour for long enough? Yes. 'That guy used to be sound but ever since he got that Tesla he's become a complete dick.' People turn into dicks through a slow, grinding process of committing dickish acts on a daily basis. It's very sad.

HE COULD BE A DUMBASS

Dumbass is an American term that is applied to all those doing stupid things. As such, a person can be a gobshite, an idiot, a dick, a knob, a spanner, a dope or a douche while simultaneously being a dumbass. Dumbass is more of an umbrella term for those who do not behave with any thought for others. 'Some dumbass unplugged the internet while I was booking concert tickets.' Dumbass is a far milder term than any of the aforementioned tags. Men will regularly apologise to their partner for stupid shit they have done by citing their propensity to be a dumbass. 'I was such a dumbass at the wedding. I don't know what came over me.' A person who acts like a dumbass at times is far from a lost cause. It's more of a glitch in their system, one that we are all prone to experience at times. Some may even find it adorable and therein lies the danger. (See the chapter on gobshites in relationships.)

HE COULD BE A TWERP

Twerp and dweeb are first cousins. A twerp is a more snivelling and cunning creature than a gobshite or any of the individuals labelled above. Twerps have a confidence about themselves that is unjustified. They move through the world with a certain air of entitlement and superiority, as if they know something you don't know. 'What is with this twerp?' is a sentence you will regularly hear in relation to these people. Twerps are far from stupid but there is an ignorance to them. Twerps have no loyalty and are completely self-serving. They like nothing more than to advance themselves at your expense. A twerp will have you help them move house and then refuse to answer their phone when they know you need the same favour. A twerp looks at your Instagram stories but never comments or likes anything. Twerps often get jobs working in the public service.

HE COULD BE A DOUCHE OR DOUCHEBAG

A douche and the bag attached to it was originally a device for colonic irrigation. Spraying water up a dirty butthole and collecting the remaining faecal matter and shit liquid is a job nobody wants to think about. And yet some genius in America saw this piece of equipment and thought, 'I know a guy just like this!' Douchebags are a law unto themselves. A douchebag is a thoughtless individual who believes themselves to be a lot of fun while constantly upsetting everyone around them. 'That douchebag who's laughing over there, yeah that one. He just pissed on the seat of my bicycle.' 'These douchebags are refusing to leave the soft play area, should we call the cops?' 'Stop being a douche, give him back the baseball and apologise to the child you shoved.' On the surface they appear to be gobshites; they tick a lot of the boxes. But there is one key difference. Gobshites are at times lovable. People fall for gobshites. I know it seems odd but some people genuinely find gobshites attractive on some level. They fall in love. They get married – often to other gobshites – but the point is they get married. Douchebags, by contrast, are impossible to love. They remain single or have a series of short-term toxic relationships. You've probably seen them on *Judge Judy* arguing over a debt they left with an ex-girlfriend. If you or someone you know is in a relationship with a douchebag, now is the time to arrange an intervention. This will not end well.

A BIT OF A GOBSHITE – NOT A COMPLETE GOBSHITE

I would argue that this category is a false narrative provided by those unfortunate enough to be in love with a gobshite or, worse, the mother of one. Saying someone is a bit of a gobshite is a contradiction in terms. A gobshite is not something you can 'sort of' be. You either are or you are not a gobshite. It's like racism. You can't say racist things and not be a racist. You can't be a little bit racist. If anything you say or do could be regarded as racist, that makes you a racist. If you are engaged in gobshite practices you are a gobshite. There are no partial gobshites, just people who don't accept that the person they are dealing with is a gobshite. It's nice to hold out hope for a person, but I think over the past few chapters we have started to come to terms with the gobshite state of being. It's a way of life. Unlike an eejit or any of the labels above, there is no half-way house with gobshites. They exist as beings so different and bizarre to the rest of us that this book was needed to unpick their habits and traits so that we might better co-exist with them.

Gobshites are not the only upsetting people in this world. In the next diagram, we can see the most common groups and how their intersection forms other wildly annoying subcategories. What is also contained in this graph is an of understanding of what makes the gobshite so uniquely upsetting. As you can see, the gobshite is neither a complete dope nor an arse/arsehole. They exist outside of the parameters of conventional odd balls as we know them. They are a cross between a head melter, and a total eejit and an absolute spanner. The intersection of all three sets is what gives them their complete incompetence and waster sensibilities.

Many but not all gobshites will be wrongly labelled. Why not recreate this handy diagram on cue card, laminate it and carry it around for those baffling moments at work or with the family when you wonder, 'Is this person a gobshite?'

Gobshite Venn Diagram

Odd Balls

Morons   Saps

Plebs

Eejits   Wankers   Head
Melters

Gobshites

Completely
Incompetent   Tools   Knobs

Langers   Dicks

Dopes   Arses

Planks   Pricks

Spanners

27

What Can We Learn from Gobshites?

'That gobshite can't take a hint, can he?' 'When is that gobshite going to leave? Everyone is in their pyjamas.' 'Is that gobshite still out there trying to build a snowman? It's minus 20 degrees.'

When a gobshite puts their mind to something their determination is as relentless as their whistling. The problem is, a lot of the time the things they become determined to do are a complete waste of time. Like sweeping leaves on a windy day, scrolling through brain rot on TikTok, seeing how loud they can make their shoes squeak or putting neon lights under the wheel arches of their cars. But what if we harnessed the dogged, resilient power of the gobshite? What if we were able to focus their numbskull energy towards something positive? Could gobshites have a positive impact on our homes, workplaces and the community?

If we took a typical gobshite, one who, like so many gobshites, is oblivious to social cues such as when to leave a house they are visiting, could we employ him to do something where that gormless nature would be useful? Could this kind of gobshite be of service if employed to inform people of flight delays in an airport, for example? This is a role that requires a person with a complete lack of empathy, reflected in a blunt delivery that says arguing over this news is futile. Surely a typically oblivious-to-the-feelings-of-others gobshite could be helpful here?

You might be forgiven for thinking that airlines have been recruiting gobshites to man their check-in desks and baggage handling for years, but you would be wrong. Airlines did for a time positively discriminate towards hiring gobshites but found very quickly that while the gobshites were able to do some things, they failed miserably at other crucial tasks. For instance, most gobshites could successfully tell people their flight had been delayed without registering the upset this information caused the customer, but they could not be relied upon to do simpler things such as remembering their email address or login. As always, fine details pose a massive problem when employing a gobshite.

While in theory it made sense to hire gobshites to tell people bad news because they would take no emotional hit from the abuse they received, in practice gobshites hired by airlines failed spectacularly at the basics of the check-in desk job. They struggled to inform travellers of where to go next or if there was an alternative flight. They spilled coffee on their keyboards. They broke their chairs due to excessive spinning. They got sick on their keyboards due to excessive spinning. They showed up at airports where they were not employed. They arrived at bus depots thinking they were airports. These gobshites informed people their flight had been cancelled when their flight was on time and managed to create problems where problems had never existed before.

ARE GOBSHITES A CATALYST
FOR CHANGE?

To the credit of these gobshites, they have forced the
companies that hired them to improve certain aspects
of their services. Gobshites are the reason self-check-
in is standard practice in airports across the world. The
streamlining of systems, procedures and codes of practice are
mostly gobshite-driven because companies have to account
for the gobshite users, buyers, employees and customers.
Electronic bus timetables exist because gobshites found
the printed ones too complicated to read. Self-driving cars,
restaurants that insist you order by scanning a barcode, self-
check-in at hotels, automatic renewal of insurance, standing
orders, direct debits – gobshites have forced businesses to
make all our lives easier. Business and tech had to get creative
in order to avoid having to deal with gobshites fucking
absolutely everything up.

So maybe the next time you see a gobshite trying to open their
hotel room door with a bank card rather than their room key,
or a gobshite making a complete balls of cleaning a window,
take a moment and think. Will this gobshite's struggle through
life actually make things easier for me in the future? Will hotels
find a simpler way for us to enter our rooms? Will windows
clean automatically? Maybe. Or maybe a gobshite will find a
way of breaking those new innovations too.

28

Am I a Gobshite?

Gobshites rarely have the capacity to reflect. You rarely see a gobshite sitting at a window pensively gazing into the distance with a brandy, mulling over their life's path. The fact that you are asking yourself, 'Am I a gobshite?' is a very good sign. Were you raised by gobshites? Are all your siblings gobshites? Are you concerned it might run in the family? Have you just realised that all your friends are gobshites and you're worried that you've spent so much time with them that unbeknown to yourself, you have become a gobshite too? With this handy test you can figure out if the worst has happened.

TAKE THE GOBSHITE TEST

1) **Have you heard people refer to you as a gobshite?**
   a. Yes, all the time.
   b. Sometimes, but only when I'm rollerblading.
   c. I occasionally get asked, 'Are you some kind of gobshite?'
   d. No, never.

2) **Has a parent or guardian defended your behaviour in the past?**
   a. No. I have a solicitor who looks after all the complaints that get made against me each month.
   b. Yes. They are always telling people 'I meant well'.
   c. I'd have to ask my mother.
   d. No. Never.

3) Do you regularly say any of the following sentences?

'Ah, I think you're being fierce hard on me.'

'I was drunk. You can't blame me for that.'

'I suppose this is all my fault again, is it?'

'It's a joke. Everyone's gone so serious.'

'It was like that when I got here.'

a. Yes to all of the above. (It's like you're reading my mind.)

b. Only when I'm repeating back what my brother says to me.

c. Some of them.

d. No, never.

4) Do you find yourself regularly leaving phone messages?

a. No. A lot of people seem to have my number blocked.

b. Yes. Nobody ever seems to pick up the phone to me.

c. No. I just repeatedly text people until eventually they stop reading my messages.

d. No.

5) How did your last romantic relationship end?

a. I'm not really sure. I think I am in a relationship but she's not answering the phone.

b. Apparently I cheated on her but I have no recollection of that night.

c. They went mental.

d. We just outgrew each other. Went our separate ways.

6) Do you get asked to take care of things by friends and family?

a. Not since the incident.

b. The only time I get asked to 'take care of things' is when I have messed something up and I'm expected to go back to the hotel or wherever and apologise to the person who is mad at me.

c. I don't get asked but I always try to do nice things for people and then they get mad at me.

d. Yes. I'm always getting asked to help people move, house sit or help with things.

7) How many fines, late fees, penalties or warning letters have you received this year?
   a. My mother handles all that stuff for me.
   b. Couldn't put a number on it, it's constant.
   c. I got one scary one last month. I paid it and cancelled the direct debit.
   d. None.

8) Have you ever been removed from an event?
   a. Bouncers seem to have it in for me.
   b. Do you count weddings in this? If so, yes.
   c. I have been removed from several nightclubs but I've always found a way back in.
   d. Never.

9) What's your opinion of health and safety nowadays?
   a. Health and safety are the two words I hear the most when I'm being removed from events.
   b. The world has gone mad.
   c. I feel like a lot of it is about preventing people from having any craic.
   d. I feel like health and safety was not a concern when I was kid but it is now.
   e. Is this a trick question?

10) Which of the following words are used to describe your personal hygiene?
    a. Do you get a smell off me?
    b. Overpowering.

c. Musty.

d. Meticulous.

11) You have been paid to do a day's fence painting in advance. Halfway through painting the fence you realise that you do not have enough paint to complete the job. What do you do?

    a. Immediately stop and go to the pub. Not your fault and you have the money.

    b. Sit and wait while playing games on your phone until someone comes along to check on how you're doing. Then you can explain that you were reluctant to keep going because you had so little paint.

    c. Water down the paint and complete the job. It might look shite but nobody will notice.

    d. Use the money you were paid to buy extra paint. Complete the job and ask to be reimbursed.

12) How do family functions tend to play out in your house?

    a. Confusing. They always start with people warning me what I shouldn't say or do.

    b. Zero fun. I feel like I'm the only one who is up for a laugh in my family and yet 90 per cent of the time people are angry with me. I'm never sure why!

    c. Fine. There's always loads of food and drink for me so I'm happy out.

    d. Great. I love getting to see my family and catch up.

13) How would you describe your financial situation?

    a. Dire. Pints are too expensive these days. The government is doing nothing about it.

    b. Solid. My mother puts money into my account each month.

    c. Precarious. Doesn't matter how many times I pay the fines, there's always more of them.

    d. Relatively stable. I have some savings and a steady
       enough income.

14) **Which of these best describes your idea of a relaxing afternoon?**
    a. Pints in a pub, followed by more pints in another pub,
       followed by chips somewhere.
    b. I don't know, just like a day where people aren't on my case
       about what I did or what I said yesterday. A day where I'm
       just allowed a rest from hearing about my past fuck-ups.
    c. A day where I don't have to deal with my gobshite's shit.
       Just one day. That would be heaven to me.
    d. Going for a pleasant walk in a picturesque area.
       Stopping for coffee or lunch with friends.

15) **To what extent do you keep up to date with the news and current affairs?**
    a. I don't understand the question.
    b. I find the news boring. It's always so negative except
       when they like have dogs or monkeys on doing mad
       stuff like riding a skateboard. I like that kind of news.
    c. I get all my news from TikTok.
    d. I watch the news twice a day. It's good to keep up with
       what's happening in the world.

16) **Do you believe in the paranormal?**
    a. Not just the paranormal. I am absolutely positive there
       are aliens that have made contact with us and a lot of
       people in Mullingar will back me up on this.
    b. Oh God yeah. I have multiple mad stories about lads
       seeing ghosts when they were half pissed.
    c. Yes – I'm sceptical but I feel like there has to be
       something out there.
    d. No.

17) **What is the worst reaction you have ever had to a gift you gave someone?**

    a. Apparently tampons are not a good gift even though she's always banging on about them.

    b. They refused to unwrap it / said it was too late.

    c. They asked for the gift receipt.

    d. People tend to like my gifts. I love putting a lot of thought into them.

18) **Homer Simpson is...**

    a. The greatest cartoon character of our time. I have a tattoo of him on my shoulder.

    b. Someone I relate to heavily.

    c. I don't watch cartoons. I'm not a child, for God's sake.

    d. An absolute idiot who reminds me of my brother.

19) **How many times a week does someone say to you, 'What were you thinking?'**

    a. Five to ten.

    b. At my weekly disciplinary meeting in work.

    c. One or two.

    d. I can't remember the last time I heard that phrase but I say it to my husband all the time.

20) **How did you find this book?**

    a. I don't read. Someone else is reading this test out to me.

    b. Four separate people gave me a copy and said I need to read this.

    c. This book keeps getting shoved into my bag. I don't know who keeps putting it there.

    d. I don't own this book, I saw my sibling reading it and I thought I would have a look.

RESULTS

Mostly A

You are a gobshite. Unfortunately you are a lost cause, but please pass this book on to the people in your life so that they can learn strategies for dealing with you.

Mostly B

You have definite gobshite tendencies. Start the book again from the beginning and try to learn something this time.

Mostly C

Probably not a gobshite, but possibly an eejit.

Mostly D

You are not a gobshite, but you probably have to deal with one regularly. Keep fighting the good fight.

Acknowledgements

This book would not have been possible without all the gobshites who have surrounded me my entire life. What's amazing is that it was only when I sat down to write *The Gobshite Guidebook* that I realised how many of them there are. My whole life has been one long journey through swarms of gobshites – at school, in work, out and about on these chaotic streets. Gobshites have tested me and my patience on a daily basis, from my first day in pre-school when a young gobshite poured sand down the back of my T-shirt, to this day, as I write this waiting for the person in the room next door to stop humming. When I was just eight years old a gobshite child who lived nearby convinced me to ransack my father's hay barn and kick in a window to escape the mess. I'm grateful to this gobshite for showing me the path I wanted to avoid. Most of all I am grateful to my parents for recognising that I had been misled by this gobshite and that I was not the leader of that two-man gobshite rampage. Writing this book gave me an opportunity to reflect, something I am also very grateful for. Sarah Liddy and the team at Gill Books encouraged me to pursue this simple idea further and further and the fertile gobshite soil suddenly appeared. Jennifer Powell helped me understand publishing and made me believe in the value of the book's concept when she recounted to me the level of gobshitery she had been forced to cope with for the last 40 years.

I will never be able to fully thank my wife Tina for all her help in not only writing this book but in ignoring some of my gobshite behaviour in the early years of our relationship.

Many of her friends spent hours trying to convince her that I was in fact a gobshite. She has confessed that at times – mostly birthdays, Valentine's Days and at Christmas – she did find herself wondering if the recessive Regan gobshite gene was present in me. But Tina has a wealth of experience in dealing with gobshites in her own career, childhood, and immediate and extended family. She has been an extraordinary help in soundboarding the chapters, ideas and theories contained within this book. Her guidance in identifying the fine details of true gobshite behaviour was invaluable. Her radar for truth has always been highly sensitive and ultra reliable. Together we make a parenting podcast specifically about raising your kids not to be gobshites. It's called 'Honey! You're Ruining Our Kid'. Tina's background in early learning and child behaviour forms the backbone of the podcast and is, I believe, the main reason she has been able to put up with me all these years. Her ability to love me in spite of all the evidence that points to me being a gobshite in eejit's clothing never fails to amaze me. I don't know if anyone in this world has had to cope with more gobshite-related frustration than Tina, but like Maya Angelou said, 'still I rise.' I love you, Tina, and I hope you know this by now.

I have been blessed to have had almost three decades working with the gobshites of the entertainment industry. Entertainment attracts individuals that in any other sector would be written off as unemployable gobshites of the worst kind. Entertainment, and comedy specifically, says, 'No, we can use you. We like the cut of your gobshite jib. Come on in. Everyone shut up and listen to this gobshite speak into this microphone. Or better still, have a job as agent, manager and booker. Why don't you become the gobshite in charge of deciding which gobshites the world gets to see on their television?' Some of the gobshites I have encountered in my time in the business will never know how much help they were in the writing of this book. Even if they read this, which they won't, they will never recognise themselves in any of the chapters. The gobshites running comedy clubs who let the audience get on stage and lick my face – you pushed me to get the hell out of those rooms. The gobshites who thought it was okay to pay the comedians the same amount in 2025 as they did in 1996 – you continue to set the bar for infuriating gobshitery where there's nothing we can do about it. The gobshite comedian who told me not to look him in the eye when I passed him on stage – you opened those eyes to the level of ignorance a gobshite could hope to reach. The gobshites who tried to convince me that there is no demand for my humour – the moment I chose to ignore those gobshite voices was the moment my life changed. Joe Wilkinson presents himself as a gobshite on stage and screen, but as a friend and writing partner he also helped me to believe.

The true power of the gobshite is not to wind you up, make you see red or force you to leave the organisation, neighbourhood, country or business. The true power of the gobshite is to show us who we don't want to be. They set an example for us all as to how not to act, how not to behave, how not to drive a taxi, raise kids, slurp soup, run a holiday home, a government or spiss-up in a brewery. The joy I have learned to extract from encountering gobshites in every corner of my life was hard won. It takes a long time and a Zen-like calm to reach a level of presence and consciousness in which you don't see gobshites as a reason to punch yourself in the dick or vagina, but rather as hilarious characters pointing us all in a more positive direction. I genuinely hope that this book can help you get there. Or if you're like me and each day brings a new challenge to your hair-trigger temper,

Acknowledgements

I hope this book can bring you back to your centre. There are gobshites in this world and there is no reaching or helping them. All we can hope to do is to navigate the challenges they pose, avoid employing them and take steps to limit the damage and heartache they cause us.

When you bring a child into this world you are terrified they will be born a gobshite and no matter what you do, the dye is cast. I'm blessed with my son, who is, if anything, less of a gobshite than me. I want to take a moment to thank Michael for inspiring me to write, work harder than I've worked before and for the coffee walks where we put the world to rights.

The past five years have seen the rise of a new kind of super gobshite. A juiced up mega gobshite who has somehow become more wealthy and more powerful than ever. These gobshites can make you feel sad and alone. They can make you throw your hat on the ground and think, this can't be it. Comedy has always been about bringing people together and laughing at things we thought that only we observed. I'm grateful to all the people who have watched my clips on Instagram, Facebook, TikTok and YouTube, who helped me realise that I'm not alone in what I think is funny. And I'm also grateful to the odd gobshite who jumps on there to tell us all we're wrong and they're right. My hope is that the next time you hear a gobshite speaking, the next time you find yourself relying upon a gobshite or married to a gobshite, this book provides you with some relief and maybe even a bit of hope. There's more of us than there are of them.

Jarlath